MASTER LUNDY'S HAPKIDO

MASTER LUNDY'S HAPKIDO

A SOLDIER'S JOURNEY

CARLTON LUNDY

MASTER LUNDY'S HAPKIDO
A SOLDIER'S JOURNEY

iUniverse books may be ordered through booksellers or by contacting:

iUniverse
1663 Liberty Drive
Bloomington, IN 47403
www.iuniverse.com
1-800-Authors (1-800-288-4677)

ISBN: 978-1-5320-0938-9 (sc)
ISBN: 978-1-5320-0939-6 (hc)
ISBN: 978-1-5320-0937-2 (e)

Library of Congress Control Number: 2016917483

Print information available on the last page.

iUniverse rev. date: 12/08/2016

PREFACE

I was a Master Sergeant in the US Air Force (USAF) military police, serving at the tail end of the Vietnam War and during the first Gulf War (Desert Storm). I take great pride in being a career veteran. I'm so proud to have been a member of the elite group of the airmen in the Strategic Air Command (SAC) during the Cold War era. I was one of the first of the all-volunteer service. We are considered the best fighting force the country has ever fielded.

Born in Virginia, I was raised in New York City. In Virginia, I attended and graduated from the Hampton Roads Regional Academy for Corrections and Law Enforcement and hold certificates of completion from both.

I have an extensive police background. I've served as a police patrol officer, port police officer, campus police, deputy sheriff, and military officer as a security specialist. My police background helped to determine my martial arts perspective.

My law enforcement background played a major role in the development of my defensive tactics. Practical techniques and their application—rather than sports tactics—were treasured and appreciated. My martial arts development became more of a combative art form as a result. It was very basic and practical.

I have served in the local school system as an educator. I've been a teacher and substituted in the local school system in Hampton and Newport News, Virginia. I have taught in the local school system at all levels from elementary to high school.

Presently I hold degrees from the Community College of the Air Force, Plattsburgh State University, and Los Angeles Community College. I also hold a master's degree in education from Strayer University.

I'm the founder of the first traditional Hapkido program at Langley Air Force Base (AFB) in Virginia. I served at Langley as the head Hapkido instructor for over twenty-five years. Teaching there has been great. I have met some of the finest people in the world from all walks of life. The military offers me a diverse group of people.

I've been blessed to have studied under and certified by some of the legendary Hapkidoists in the world: Park Son Han of Kunsan and Myung Kwang Sik, the "O" brothers in Kunsan, South Korea, both senior masters. I studied briefly under Master Kim of Daegu (K-2) of South Korea. These masters were some of the best Hapkido masters in Korea at the time.

I believe the people I have met over the years was all preparation for the classroom of life. South Korea was where I studied predominately. I've never had an American instructor. The South Korean masters played a major role in my adult development. Most of my young adult life was spent in South Korea in increments. I served four tours there.

I value teaching as a calling and not an occupation. Teaching is not easy and not for everyone. Loving learning, I have made it a lifelong endeavor. While traveling in the military, I became fascinated by different cultures and languages.

I now put great value on observing different points of view. I'm diverse in my thought processes. I'm extremely grateful to the South Korean people for nurturing me spiritually and emotionally. The strong cultural values and discipline I have encountered over the years has been motivational. Today these cultural influences and ethics have shaped me.

My wife (Sun Yong)—or Annie as I knew her—was a native South Korean and the love of my life. We learned each other's language together. I learned to speak Korean, and she learned to speak English from a Korean English dictionary. I still have it. We learned to respect each other's culture. It was the backbone of our relationship. We shared common social issues. We raised two grown children, our two lovely daughters, Freda and Angie. I dedicate this book to them.

I hope to one day remarry again. If God wills it, I will. I'm hopeful that one day I'll become a grandfather and enjoy the company of my grandchildren. I aspire to live to see my daughters marry.

I would like to help and serve others. I was born to serve. I'd like nothing better than to continue to share my skills with the youth and adult population of the world. I love teaching and interacting with people. As a servicemen I feel it is my duty as an American to pass on some of the many experiences.

I have arranged the book for a martial arts audience and an audience who likes a good story. For my former students, pay close attention to the names of the chapters. To the second group, look for changes in styles as a result of certain social situations. For one group, I hope they like a good story. Both audiences can enjoy a smooth ride and a good story.

The chapters are arranged and named with ten chapter titles. Each chapter has subtitles to highlight certain social events that dominated the situation at the time. My students will hopefully recognize the names of the techniques that have changed my life. I'm hoping you will enjoy a marvelous journey called *Master Lundy's Hapkido*.

INTRODUCTION

This book is dedicated to my two lovely
daughters Freda and Angie

Master Lundy's Hapkido is an autobiography, a memoir, and
a soldier's story. It's my legacy. I used every tool in my toolbox
that life presented me. Sometimes I received amazing results
in life. Some of the situations looked impossible at first. It's a
story of survival. It's a tale of how nothing is impossible through
persistence, determination, and a love of God.

This story outlines the qualities of a rich man. How do you
get paid for what you like to do? You turn ordinary things such
as a hobby into a lifetime commitment. It's a story of how to use
martial arts to serve mankind.

It's a memoir and autobiographic in describing how a man-
child learned to become a better man. It's the story how a young

man's thirst for survival led to unshakable courage and enthusiasm. While I learned to live in a parentless situation, the world became my classroom. It's a book of how to help others obtain their dreams and aspirations.

The story covers the journey from a small town in Virginia and then takes you through the streets of Spanish Harlem in New York City. It covers my military experiences. You will travel to South Korea and back.

The journey included service as an amateur boxer, master sergeant in the USAF, city patrol officer, port police officer, correctional officer, schoolteacher, author, martial arts master, husband, and father. Take my hand and walk with me through adventure after adventure.

Master Lundy's Hapkido brings a picture from the rim of failure to several pentacles of success. The story covers how God makes warriors both physical and spiritual for influencing others. It's the account of how Master Lundy was equipped for spiritual warfare. It's a tale of how I became a soldier in the army of the Lord.

My family and moral fortification are the guiding light in all my endeavors. I have arranged the book for both a martial arts audience and a reader who likes a good story. Certain names and identifying characteristics have been changed. I thank God for my journey.

CHAPTER 1

TURNING LEAF

Technique #1

The Making of a Strong Man, Grandma, Ma, and My Older Sister

Picture of three generations of women in my life:
my mother, oldest sister, and grandmother

I was born in the small town of Jarratt, Virginia, in 1954. Dwight D. Eisenhower was the president at my birth. One of his favorite quotes, spoken by Mark Twain, said, "It's not the size of the dog in the fight; it's the size of the fight in the dog." This statement might sum up my attitude at a very young age when I was an aggressive individual.

My hometown is one of those places where you reference it to another town, which is now the city of Emporia, Virginia. Jarratt was seven miles from Emporia.

When I was between four and six years of age, one of my nephews started a fire, and the house burned down. This was somewhat traumatic for someone my age. But boys will be boys. The story goes that one of my nephews was playing with matches under the bed. He lit up the cotton mattress that was overhead, and of course, the more we fanned it, the bigger it got. Three of us were at the location. I was there but didn't strike the match. We were fortunate no one was hurt. We were negligent and ignorant kids.

So we burned down the house. I don't think my people owned the home either. Off we went to move to a new location. At that time, it was my mother, me, and one of my sister's three kids.

Our neighbors were harassed by us doing boyish things like dirt fights. Once the ground was plowed for gardens in the spring, we played with it. We used the sod for ammunition to throw and have dirt fights. My nephews and I loaded up sod. Semidry, it made great dirt bombs. We stacked up the dirt for ammunition, which we needed ammunition for war on the neighborhood. Then we took up fortifications and began to fire at each other at will. It was a big war game with two families on each side, like the Hatfields and the McCoys. It's funny how something this simple thing has survived in my memory for all of these years. When I look back, we were some busy little kids we got into a lot of things and needed close supervision.

These were my earliest memories of the new home. I must have been between four and seven years of age at that time. These are some of my strongest memories of early childhood in Virginia.

My mother was a single parent with three grown children. When I was little, she had been married once, and my first three siblings had the same father. Then there was me and my little sister. We both had different fathers. I never knew mine. My oldest sister had two sons and a girl that my mom took care of. She had quite a crew on her hands.

My mother kept my sister's children while she traveled north to find work in New York City. My oldest brother was already there, working as a truck driver. Most people in our town during that time longed to leave home and head north for work, where there were opportunities and a better way of life. This was a common experience for blacks at that time in the South. Thousands of young people of that era split as soon as possible to the major cities. Today I like to tell people that African Americans can identify with the Mexican immigrants in their search for employment. Our family, like others, were willing to travel to help support family: Detroit, Chicago, New York, Cleveland, and Tennessee. Any city with job opportunities would do. How soon we forget about our journeys to prosperity. It looks like the same tactic to me.

My middle sister was married with her own children. She lived in the town with my mother. If you were a single parent and had to raise a family by yourself, this would have been a giant task. Large and extended families were a necessity for survival.

I never knew my biological father personally. I know I had a different last name. I carry the name today of my mother's first husband. There are lots of African American families in the same boat. If you are not careful, you could marry a sister or brother if you live in a small town somewhere.

My oldest sister's son was my best friend. We were three months apart. I think they saw them—my father and her first husband—in my nephew and me. I think that was why the grown- ups liked to see my nephew and me wrestle all the time when company came.

My nephew and I were great competitors our whole lives. During our teenage years, we were both captains. If we played on the same side, our contemporaries were destined to lose. We were like two leaders in all we did. He would later join the marines. I became a career airmen in the USAF.

Mom had me and my little sister and then an infant. The two of us had different fathers. I never really knew my father's side of the family. They were in that town or near there somewhere. Bless them wherever they are. After learning later what happened there, I wonder how they could have still stayed there in that small town. The only industry besides sharecropping was working in somebody's house. That's the way things were.

I understood the situation. I did not like the situation even as a child. I now think of my story as a history lesson for many other African American families of the time. We all start out at the same point. Most were raised in extended families.

When we were very young, we thought we were all brothers and sisters. We thought we just had a lot of mothers. When I was young, I think my mom had a "shot house" too. This is where liquor was sold without a license. This was risky because you could be put in jail. With all those young children, how could you do any time? At my age at the time, how could I say or not tell what was going on?

Working in someone's house might have been the only sense of security a young person might have. Today I think how family structures have changed. Technology has greatly transformed the family. People would rather text than talk to family. Back then, family depended on each other.

My uncle and his family lived nearby on a farm, but it was not their farm. They were sharecroppers, that is, they would share the yields of the crops by tending the land. It was a rough system. Thank God it was finally broken. This was on my mother's side of the family. We called it "over the river."

Our uncle had two children, but they had huge families. Until this day I don't think I know all of them. They had a lot of children so they could help the family work. They didn't make much money. The more kids they had, the more help they had.

My parents made sure we knew who was our family in most cases. Many family secrets were in those woods. My family was not any different than most. I was to learn many secrets. I've been told that minerals were found on the land and that system was broken. Hallelujah!

Like I said, my older brother was already in New York City. My oldest sister was to join him, but not in the same house or borough, as we call cities in New York City. A borough could be called a specific district in a very large city. New York City consisted of five boroughs but in the same city. My brother always lived in Brooklyn. My eldest sister was in Manhattan and then later in the Bronx. The rest of the known family lived in Virginia then. My brother and sister were the first to migrate to the city.

During our early years, my sister's daughter was the oldest. She was about two years older than us. She used to try to play "mamma." When my mom left the house, she was in charge. She tried to whip us with a branch from a tree or bushes. Her brother chased her with a wooden axe. She was only about ten or maybe twelve, trying to play "Mother." Bless her. She was just trying to help.

Then there were the two younger members. My baby sister was an infant. My oldest sister's son was next youngest. When I think of it, Mom had quite a job. Where you saw one, you would see the other.

At a young age, we all had huge characters. We played poker, or we thought we could. The younger son, the little guy who made everybody laugh, was two years younger than us. Even to this day, he is still the best joker in the family. At that time, our ages seemed to be large differences. It seems so insignificant now. Wow! I think we all developed this joking skill as a defense mechanism. We got good at it. To this day, we all have the gift. I realize now how traumatic these experiences are on children.

My oldest sister would visit on major holidays and times. We were later to join her in New York with her common-law husband, who would later become her husband and the only father figure most of us ever knew at that time.

One day my mother told us that we were moving to New York City—indoor plumbing, showers, new schools, and bright lights. We didn't know what to expect. We were very happy to move to New York City.

My middle sister had three boys, and they lived in a neighboring town. We left her there with her family. My sister sent for us. At that time she was separated from her spouse as well. It must have been pretty hard on her as a women at that time.

We were now leaving the country roads of Virginia for the bright lights of New York City to join my oldest sister. We stayed in another house before we settled in Spanish Harlem. I think we were in Black Harlem prior to moving to our six-room apartment in Spanish Harlem.

I like to compare this part of my life to a turning leaf. The social opportunity to transform from country living to city life were huge. My view of life and its perspective were to change forever. In my Hapkido class, the first grappling technique we learned is called "turning leaf" or technique number one. The person is standing in front, and you want to take him or her down. You take his hand and bring it across his body while blocking, causing him to be unable to attack. Then you step under and through, causing him to somersault. Then you add the master's touch. You use the knee on the back of his elbow while turning his palm face-down to the ground with both hands at a forty-five-degree angle. If executed with more than the slightest amount of pressure, it will cause serious wrist and elbow damage. Don't attempt without trained supervision.

Socially speaking, my mother, older sister, and grandmother were major players in my early life. At this time, their lives were being turned upside-down. Grandma has passed. Later in life, I learned I was in her arms when she passed. My oldest sister told me that she was a teacher. I don't remember much of that, but I do know I have taught on many levels and I love teaching. I've been trained formally as an educator.

Things were changing for the better. They were starting to turn. We were en route to the big city. I knew my mother must have been glad. My sister also must have been glad to join her family. We were leaving "turning leaf" and heading on to the next chapter, the "revolving door."

CHAPTER 2

REVOLVING DOOR

Technique #2

Living between Manhattan, Brooklyn, and the Bronx

the subway; my mode of transportation from my youth

We moved to 126 East 118th Street in Harlem. These were some of the best times of my young life. We lived on the sixth floor. No elevator was in the building. We didn't care. The steps made me a good athlete. I was one of the fastest kids on the block because of those steps. I could climb them like an antelope. The smell of garlic in the air, all in the hallway, made us stronger as we climbed those stairs. In the summer, the smell got stronger the higher we climbed.

In the summer, to cool off, the kids used the fire hydrants. We'd get a soda or beer can, one that had been scrapped on both ends to hollow it so we could shoot the water hydrant on hot days. If we held it with both hands and let it down on the spray slowly, we could control the high pressure it was under.

If we weren't fast, they would get us with the pump. That water was ice-cold. We could get knocked off our feet and moved under a car or something. The spray could reach two or three stories high. We would get excited.

"Go get your bathing suit! The pump is on!"

I think we got the idea from the fire hoses they were using on people in the South. During that time, I didn't see the association. We knew what water pressure could do, so we played with it.

We had high-rise apartment buildings at least five and six stories up. None had elevators. The pump was next to our apartment entrance. When it was on, people tried to wet us. The whole neighborhood was in danger.

All of the buildings had fire escapes. Some had a fire escape on the front; others had adjoining roofs. That's what the hydrants were for. When the the hydrants ran too much in the summer, the water would come up rusty, and they would put a sprinkler cap on them. The Police Athletic League did it. We didn't like the sprinkler. It was not dramatic enough. We wanted the water hose, like what we saw on the news during the civil rights movement.

Our street was a play street. During the summer, cars were not allowed on our street. The police designated it as closed off. No traffic could come through. We played all day in safety under a neighbor's watchful eye. That didn't stop the cursing. I think we learned it from some of the adults, like Kiddy on the second floor. An Italian lady was always out the window and talking stuff.

The men in our family would be on the corner watching us, like my brother-in-law and our friends' parents. And there was my brother-in-law and his brother. Mr. Sheppard, our adopted extended family from Virginia, was our second father. A man we called nicknamed "Big Man" was always looking out for us also.

The salesmen were the heroin addicts. They were always stealing and selling stuff "hot," as we called it. They broke into homes too. Sometimes we'd bomb them with eggs from the roof or water balloons. That was why we always walked under those fire escapes when on the street. If you got hit from six stories up with something, it might be fatal.

The corner was also the point where they could get the number from a lookout we all knew. The number runner could be caught while on the run. The local heroin addicts also sold merchandise on this point. It was stolen merchandise, anything from clothes to TVs.

Some days we might catch a junkie, or heroin addict, in a deep nod. Then we'd slap one and make him chase us. Dudley would probably do something like that. If you asked him, he would do it. He was only about five years old at the time and could cuss like a sailor. The adults used to pay him to cuss out someone. He was so good you would beg him to stop. He was part of our family.

One time I had to hide under a parked car for about a half hour before I could double back home. This guy chased us all day. When I finally made it up the six flights of stairs, I looked out the window. He was still looking for us.

Most were neighborhood people we knew or sometimes someone who came from other places to buy drugs. It was dangerous to be on our block if you didn't live there or were not invited. You had to know your areas like the back of your hands.

At good old 126th, I went up the stairs like an antelope. I went to look out the window to look at them fools high on drugs. We didn't know most by name. It must have been hard on Mom at her age.

I soon became the fastest runner in the neighborhood. Day in and day out, I climbed those stairs at a high rate of speed. Sometimes you had to run; other times you had to make a stand. When you hit the steps, you were close to home.

I must be truthful. I was not afraid to run sometimes. I was the fastest kid on the block. Those stairs made me strong. The neighborhood was very dangerous. At times we had to go back downstairs and take care of business. There was no running home crying. If we had to go back downstairs, somebody was getting his butt kicked. You can't go home when it's serious business.

I was pretty good with my hands, also at a young age. I had no formal training. You had to know how to fight. Honor and respect was an issue in our upbringing in the neighborhood. In Spanish Harlem at that time, if someone said "your mother" or "you faggot," those were automatic fighting words. This meant you were a homosexual. Today they don't have the same meanings.

In Harlem, you had to learn to protect yourself at an early age. You could get a fair fight if everybody knew each other. You were jumped if you didn't. This was reserved for only those who have earned it. If not, you had to know how to street fight. You had to know how to hold your hands up high. I had a technique where I would slap down their hands, exposing them to an overhand right. That usually did it, right in the face. If not, I knew how to wrestle from TV. The gut shot was a warning. Profanity was a weapon also. Dudley had it down to a science.

For life-threatening situations, we'd use bottles or anything we could get your hands on, especially garbage can tops, sticks, and pipes. Street Survival 101 was the game, and these were the primary weapons. You didn't have to win every fight, but you had to fight.

You had to know someone who knew someone on the block, or you could get jumped if you didn't. Protection was guaranteed for those who had earned it. You needed a reputation for kicking butt right. If there were anyone from another block, we all jumped in. We were all obligated to help our family and friends. This made the streets extremely dangerous. We had to stick together.

On the street, we sometimes had to schedule fights. It was a promotion to kick somebody's butt right. It was bragging rights. In a Spanish neighborhood, you sometimes would have to fight the whole family, occasionally one on one. But if they caught you wrong, you better make a point.

People were always on the steps, except at night. At night, you needed at least two people for security. On the low levels, they were behind the steps. On the higher levels, they were near the roof, taking drugs or flying pigeons. The rest was activity going between the two.

My nephew was like Lenny in *Of Mice and Men*, a big, strong fellow for his age. He was not mentally ill. I think he was too strong and he knew it. He was my constant companion who always cried when he had to fight someone. He had tough wrestling moves, like the back breaker, which we begged him not to do on somebody's father because he was only eight or ten years old. He was one of those fellows that lost it when he got mad.

Harlem life definitely turned us into street people. We learned to hold our own on those mean streets for the rest of our lives. They gave us lifetime lessons. We learned to control our emotions under stressful situations, even at school.

People were peeing behind the staircases. They threw garbage out the windows daily because they didn't want to walk downstairs. The garbage cans were on the ground floor. The smell of garlic was always thick about five in the evening when everyone was fixing dinners. It was a majority Spanish neighborhood. The garlic confirmed it. We all loved our block.

They were taking drugs on the steps behind the steps and on the roof. Harlem was full of heroin addicts at that time, and they were always in the halls near the roof where we lived, taking needles and asking for water to take their stuff.

Occasionally they would knock on our door to get water to mix their drugs. We'd see them on the steps, taking the stuff. They didn't care. Most people were afraid to tell them to get lost. Sometimes they played tricks on us. One time I traded a big nickel, a quarter, for three nickels.

If my family had something on a person, it took about five years to wear it off. They'd hammer others with the situation for life. We'd never hear the end of that situation. They would tell me, "Remember the time you gave up a quarter for fifteen cents." I thought I had a big nickel. Three nickels is definitely better than one. Then we'd have to go to the time a family member got knocked out, which led to the time when the house got burned down.

These were my nephews and family members who wouldn't let anyone forget. They never called me "Uncle" until I was in my forties. I'd like to say that this went on in every family, but I can't. That's the way it was.

It was a tight situation in our home. I lived in a six-room apartment with my sister, her future husband, and his three children from a previous marriage. There was one girl and two boys matching my older sister's children, my mother, my little sister, and me. There was the eldest son of my sister's husband. He had a middle, his second son, and there was his second oldest. O'Neil was about three years older and the big brother of the house. The two girls were no more than a year apart. They stuck together.

I never saw them argue. Also along was my sister's husband's brother, who later became one of my idols.

My brother-in-law's aunt used to visit us from time to time. They traveled from Alabama to the city for the same reasons as my family. She wanted my brother-in-law to do the same for his family. That meant taking care of his three children by his first wife. This was my mentor's aunt also.

My mentor was my brother-in-law's brother. He moved in from Detroit. He had been a boxer in his youth in Detroit. He was my idol growing up. He was always clean and had nice clothes, and he seemed to have it together. He was in his early twenties at the time. When I look back, I don't know how he wasn't drafted into the military. He was the youngest of three brothers. Perhaps because his next-to-oldest brother had served.

There was a grand total of twelve people—four adults and eight children—in one apartment. The six rooms included the bathroom and kitchen. This was not uncommon in Spanish Harlem. Our neighbor from Puerto Rico had two adults and eight children. Some of the kids went to Catholic school. Most of my friends went to public school.

Most of the family attended P.S. #7 on Lexington Avenue and 122nd Street in Harlem. My third-grade teacher was Miss Crocket. I was in love with her. She was a young African American teacher. I remember the day she broke the sad news to us that she was getting married. She even brought that bum to school. I couldn't stand him from the start.

Miss Crocket's class was for gifted students, and she tried to skip me one grade. I told Mom I didn't want to go to the fourth grade. I enjoyed my friends and really didn't want to leave them. Who needs to be skipped a grade anyway? I was one of the brightest in my classroom. I was not a nerd. I tried hard not to be one. You didn't want to be considered to be too smart. Someone might want to try to kick your butt. We went on a trip somewhere in the city every month.

I was in the fourth grade, 4-1 G, with Mrs. Bond when President Kennedy was killed. The "G" stood for gifted. I had some qualities for painting and artistic abilities, which I think were a little above average, thanks to God. Mrs. Bond was a little, plump Caucasian lady. The whole class cried when President Kennedy was killed. He was a Catholic. Most of my neighborhood was Catholic. This was smack in the middle of the civil rights era.

We all played the numbers, a tool among the poor all over New York City. Numbers were big in our community. In Harlem and all over New York City, it was like an illegal lottery for the poor made up of connected neighborhood people. You had to be careful where you put your clothes. Most of the cleaners were number holes. If you put your clothes in there, you would never see them again at that time. I hope things have changed, but likely not.

It was a sign of hope. You got paid cash on the spot and no taxes. It was community involvement. It was the relieve valve. It kept the adults from exploding in difficult times. It was a possible way out of the Ghetto. It also provided jobs for a professional under class locked out of the system. It wasn't easy growing up in Harlem in a multi-cultural society …

The numbers were based on the racing of the horse at the track, so everyone believed. They came out three times a day and three times at night. The point was you got paid cash, usually by somebody you knew. This system is still going on, which is still and will always be a part of New York City. It's basically an underground lottery.

As I grew older, I found out how important it was to the community. It was a sign of hope. You got paid cash on the spot without having to pay taxes. It was community involvement. It was the relief valve. It kept the adults from exploding in difficult times. It was a possible way out of the ghetto. It also provided jobs for a professional locked out of the system. It wasn't easy growing up in Harlem in a multicultural society.

Numbers remained a big part of some of our young lives. Quick money can ruin you. Locals paid off the numbers. They picked up the numbers. They were mostly people you could invite into your house. People often shared their good luck with them.

We called him the runner. The worst thing that could happen was for him to lose your trust. It could be fatal. Don't mess with poor people's money. I realize now that the numbers had a ray of hope attached to them for a seemingly desperate situation. It was a temporary fix for a growing economic problem.

My sister's husband came by some money. They said he hit a number. It was rumored that that was what happened. We don't know for sure. It was enough to make a down payment on a home. This was to change our lives from that point on.

The odds of winning outnumbered the chances of winning. Hitting a three-digit number was a lot worse, almost a miracle. People today play it at 7Eleven for greater odds. Sometimes things don't change much. It was a game changer.

My early life and childhood was like a turning leaf, one of the turning points in the developmental mentality I would carry forth in life. I learned to be cautious, courageous, strong, and loyal. Although I still don't gamble, I know some people who still do. I knew how to play straight poker, five-card stud, and blackjack when I was about eight or nine.

This was a can-do attitude and keen focus. For the rest of my life, I believed in attacking issues and taking care of things one time. We saw a lot of people get hurt on those streets. When I look back now, it was only a brief time in our lives, but it had a long-term effect.

We saw some of the vices on the street, and they took hold in different ways in our lives as we became adults. We took the gambling into the Bronx briefly in our teenage years. As a teenager, I knew how to play straight and draw poker. I learned to shoot dice and celo, a game using three dice. During my teenage years, we were athletic and gamblers.

The Youth Corps jobs saved us. We got jobs working as youth counsellors. We had a knack for the streets, and being athletic helped us make friends easily. For the rest of this book, I will reference a technique and associate with some life experience that has shaped a lifetime situation.

The names of the techniques will have a special effect on those who have studied under me over the years. This second lesson involves one of the techniques we call "revolving door." In life, there are some things you can't get out of. In the next chapter, we will see and hear of some social issues.

"Revolving door" is a term we use to describe another technique that impacted me as an instructor and teacher. It reminds me of the changes that took place next in my life. In my growth as a man and martial artist, the meaning and understanding of the procedure took on a special meaning.

My mom was a strong and feisty woman. There were tensions in the household, as you might imagine. Having eleven other people in one household can be challenging. We all got along extremely well under the circumstances. My mom treated us all equally, and she was like everybody's grandmother. She took care of everybody, cooking and looking after us in school. She was our guardian.

Finance was a problem. We ate a lot of beans, Spam, and cheese. I went to get the welfare systems support: the peanut butter, cheese, and powdered milk. I hated to get it. I didn't want to be seen with it. Everybody was on some kind of support, but you didn't want to say you were receiving some subsistence.

My sister and her husband both worked, but they still needed help with all the people. My brother-in law worked as well, but they needed some help with all those people and kids in one place.

My oldest sister later retired from the Bell Telephone System as a manager. My older brother, a truck driver, worked out of the garment district for most of his life. He is now deceased. My middle sister became a homemaker and great-grandmother many times over. And my youngest sister is a social worker and community activist. She still lives in Brooklyn.

My brother-in-law is a pipe fitter and plumber without certification. I realized at a young age how hard he used to work for what he earned. His knowledge exceeded his paycheck. Now retired, he is recognized as the only father figure I have ever known. I realize at this time the trouble he had with certification because of discrimination and other social problems. They did the best they could, considering the circumstances. He was a hard worker who always toiled and tried to do the right thing. They presently live in a small town, Jarratt, Virginia, and own property. Sometimes "he who laughs last laughs best." Our backgrounds help to make out successes in the future.

One time there was an argument and a fight in the house. It revolved around money. My older brother, the truck driver, came. As a result, my mom, sister, and me had to move to 658 DeKalb Avenue in the Bedford-Stuyvesant area of Brooklyn.

This was a trying time for me. I went to junior high school on Tompkins Avenue. I didn't like it very much. My mom had some friends on Pulaski Street and Marcy Avenue. For me, it was a lonely time. I missed the old gang from Manhattan.

Our home was a two-bedroom place located about two blocks from my middle sister's place. At this time, this was quite an accomplishment for my mother. All of her children were out of those woods. They had an opportunity for a better life.

It's funny that I never looked at it this way until now. This was no doubt one of her finer moments. She was on her own again. My mother was so young when she started to raise children. My younger sister and I were a young aunt and uncle to many. Maybe that made my cousin and their families so close. They would have been my mother's friends in her youth. She would have been a young aunt.

My second-oldest sister was to join us. She had an apartment on Marcy Avenue in the Stuyvesant area of Brooklyn. In New York City, she brought her boys with her from Virginia. She had a daughter, but she wasn't with her. It was a tough situation for her. Her house was near our place, maybe on Pulaski and Willoughby on Marcy Avenue in Brooklyn, a couple city blocks from us.

In 2014, I read a book that brought back those memories, Reverend Al Sharpton's *The Rejected Stone*. As a young preacher, he preached in the church across the street from my sister. At the time I had no idea. It was a rough neighborhood with the DeKalb Avenue Chaplains, the community gang.

It was surprising to learn such an icon was so near and shaped by the events of the times. These experiences has led him forward to become one of our most faithful civil rights leaders. The streets of New York City have transformed so many of us in different ways.

Because I had siblings who were grown when I was a child, it gave me a unique opportunity. It was like I was straddling two generations, that of my older brothers and sisters and their children. I could see them as sisters and brothers and not as mamma and dad. Don't get me wrong. I respected them as authority figures. Mom was my mom too. This was a special position now that I look back on it. I guess I did think much bigger than I was.

My older brother had a son and daughter who were close in age to us. We were no more than two years apart in age. They didn't call me "Uncle" then. They used other terminology.

As a kid, my brother loved Oldsmobile cars. They were sturdy and could take a bang. Maybe that was why he never got hurt when he had an accident. He drove a truck for many years. I have to admit he would work. On Monday he was on point.

My cousins all lived in Brooklyn at that time, except my older sister and her family. We were all no more than two or three years older than each other. We spent the night at each other's house on occasion. There were a lot of boys in my family at that time.

I had a cousin Walter, who also lived in Brooklyn. He had two children, a boy and girl, and his beautiful wife, Martha Ann, who 'til this day has the sweetest heart I have ever known. Occasionally we'd stay over at their house in Brooklyn.

My brother would drink heavily, and he was usually high on the weekend. He'd always come by sometimes during the week, but mostly on Saturdays. He also had a half-brother on his father's side who lived around the corner. I was told we had different fathers. My younger sister also had a different father who was also deceased. My older siblings, my brother, and two older sisters had the same father. He lived in New Jersey and had remarried.

Somehow he managed to make all the rounds. On the weekends my brother had to stay mostly in Brooklyn, but he traveled to the Bronx and Manhattan too. He knew how to drive all over to Jersey and everywhere. He even frequently came to Virginia to visit my uncle at least once a year. He'd always try to make it in the least amount of time. Later I began to realize these were strong men fighting to keep their families intact.

Maybe it was because he was a truck driver by trade. My brother always bragged about his road time. He loved to see how fast he could make it home to Virginia. As far as I knew, he was never locked up. It is possible.

We loved my brother and loved to ride with him. I went home with him when he lived in Brooklyn. He went to sleep at the light while waiting for it to change. We were unaware of his situation most of the time. When he gave us the offer to visit his home in Brooklyn, we didn't realize he had been drinking heavily. I won't say he was drunk. I'll say he was a little tired.

Depending on traffic, this was about forty-five minutes to an hourlong ride. We found out when we entered the expressway. When he turned on to the expressway, he almost hit the wall. We screamed for the next forty-five minutes until we got to Brooklyn.

We had to take the expressway to get to Brooklyn from Bronx or Manhattan. Either way, it took at least forty-five roller-coaster minutes. When he woke up, he mashed on the accelerator with his eyes closed.

Along the way, he told us, me and one of my nephews, who was eight or nine at the time, that we could walk if we didn't like his driving. So we decided to just watch and scream. Boy, did I wish I could drive. I loved him, and he loved us.

In Brooklyn, I had two girlfriends. One was next door to my middle sister's house; the other was around the corner. One was Caucasian; the other was a sister, a black girl. I liked both of them. But on the weekends, at twelve years of age, I caught the train headed to Spanish Harlem, which I had grown to love.

I was stuck in Harlem and later the Bronx. My friends and relatives were there. As a child, I was determined to keep the friendships I had with the Sheppards and my oldest sister's kids. Besides there was too much drama in my house in Brooklyn over the weekends.

I wanted to be a kid. It was like a revolving door. I learned to ride the metro or subway system one hour from Manhattan to Brooklyn or an hour and a half from the Bronx. I started when I was twelve. I was a street kid and couldn't get out of that revolving door. These friendships would last a lifetime. Mom did the best she could to satisfy her little man, me.

My older sister and her husband-to-be finally hit a number large enough to make a difference. In Harlem, that was the street lottery unofficial. It was a good-sized hit, which allowed them to buy a house up in the Bronx. My childhood friends, the adopted extended family, moved in under them. The new place, my older sister's home, was a two-family brick home. About this time, I, my little sister, and my mother had moved to Brooklyn near my older brother, Wesley.

We were staying on DeKalb Avenue. There was gang activity, but less diversity and drugs at that time. In Brooklyn, my area was diverse but predominately black. My brother lived in the East New York section of Brooklyn. My cousin Walter also lived in the Bushwick section of Brooklyn. Now most of the family was in Brooklyn.

Mom's passing was extremely hard for me to take. Mom had heart trouble. She passed in the hospital while I was in the Bronx. I was fourteen years old. My younger sister was seven at the time. I can't imagine how hard it was on her.

We had to be separated to keep from going to a group home. During my whole life, I never knew my father. All I knew at that time was that he was deceased. I went to live in the Bronx, permanently this time. My younger sister went with my middle sister in Brooklyn. My mom's loss was very hard on my younger sister and me. The split had affected our whole lives. I needed a role model.

I had five nephews living in Brooklyn. I had one cousin. The older was one year older, I think. The second was a year younger; the third was two years younger. Then there was the youngest. We hung out during the week. Except for the youngest, we all attended the Bedford Boys Club. On their street, I spent most of my time looking for my girl. My brother's son, his sister, and my cousin James lived across town.

Our adopted extended family, whom we loved, both children and adults, moved from Harlem to the Bronx with my sister's family. Even to this day, we had a very tight bond. At my sister's house, they lived downstairs, and my sister and her family were upstairs. The old gang would never be the same.

My mentor, my brother-in-law, stayed in Harlem and was married. The boxer from Cleveland was at my side when Mom died on that long walk from the funeral home. My mother, my younger sister, and I had lived in Brooklyn until her passing. For me, life was like a revolving door. Permanent changes were taking place. Now I realize how independence is so important in people's lives. Thank God I'm an American.

My martial arts students will remember technique number two called as the "revolving door." As I tell this story, I intend to talk to two audiences at the same time, my martial arts community and others.

I was in and out of Manhattan, the Bronx, and Brooklyn, all trying to be a kid. It socially was like a revolving door. Life changes things. When Mom passed, my world was rocked.

When my mom passed, my younger sister and I were split up. I went to live with one sister. She went to the other. I think I needed a strong father image for a while. This was devastating for me. I think this is what led me to search for positive black role models. I had also become an amateur boxer. I think at the time the two were related. When I became a boxer, I was fifteen or sixteen years of age.

I was in my second year of high school in gifted classes in a college bound program. I tried to do the best I could under the circumstances. My life had become like a revolving door in reverse.

After Mom's passing, I had to reverse strategies. Now it was visiting Brooklyn to see my little sister when I could. Things had changed dramatically. I looked for father images.

CHAPTER

3

THE GROIN KICK

Technique #3

Mom's Death, Boxing, Military, North Dakota, and First Overseas Assignment

My first assignment at Minot A.F.B
North Dakota (B-52, H Model)

Mom had a heart condition and arthritis. She had a hard life as a young mother really. I think my oldest sister was born when Mom was thirteen or fourteen. She was a child herself, raising her own.

Now in her later years, she was raising another set of children, my seven-year-old sister and me. Mom was hospitalized one weekend in Brooklyn. I went to the Bronx for the weekend. My niece was staying with us. My little sister was with my middle sister. I was fourteen. Mom passed in the hospital. I didn't get to see her. She was fifty years old when she passed.

In some way looking back, I was very independent. Maybe Mom knew I would be on my own. If it weren't for my sisters, my little sister and I would have been orphans. My oldest sister took me in, and my middle sister took in my sister. Before Mom died, this was my regiment.

My world was to be permanently changed. I can't explain what it means when a mother passes. Every male in the world who has been through it will tell you there is no replacement ever. I loved my mother, and I tried to help her.

I made furniture at the Boy's Club. Everything I brought home was wet. I couldn't wait to have the shellac dry. I made a planter's coffee table and bookshelves. I went to the Bronx and Manhattan a lot, but I still loved Mom. I was traveling on the metro or subway forty-five minutes to an hour and a half alone.

Mom's death was surprising and devastating. Never knowing my father put me in a nasty situation. I had to grow up as soon as possible. I did graduate from high school, William Howard Taft High School, in the Bronx. I was one of the first in my family that I knew about.

Graduating from high school presented another dilemma, some major issues that had to be addressed. This would require I either go to work full time, move on my own, or go to school. I was legally an adult at eighteen years of age. I had no money.

Through the college bound program, I was able to get into a work-study program with John Jay College of Criminal Justice in New York. I had no money. The school had a program with the city where they helped young students find work that would allow them to go to school.

I got on a work-study program that allowed me to buy my books and pay tuition and car fare to and from the job. I lived at my sister's place for the time being. This was my first year of college. I was in a special program called "Thematic Studies."

My first year of college was difficult. Remember that I was the first. I didn't have any mentors. I was taking courses in a random fashion. I had a guidance counselor, bless her soul, in high school, but now I was in college. I was in the world now. If you make a mistake, I hope you learned from it. The air force and Minot were next.

My little sister and I were split up. I went to my older sister to keep from being sent to a children home ran by the state. She went to our middle sister. Looking back, I think of my little sister. She was seven. Whatever I felt, she must have gotten it double.

My younger sister, I believe, is still traumatized to this day. She was seven and never knew her dad. I was fourteen. We didn't want to, but things changed for all of us in our little group. I still wanted to be a kid, but destiny required a man-child.

I think I found out after I got back home from the weekend in the Bronx. My niece was living with us at that time. I was crushed. Zack and me were walking and talking after we left the funeral home in Brooklyn. My niece later married and moved to the Bronx. I was already very independent. Now I became a man-child.

When I was in high school, I spent a year in an all-boys high school in Brooklyn called Boy's High while living with my mom. It was famous for its athletics. They won the city championships in basketball, track, and football. I was proud to be there. I was in the college bound program there. After Mom's death, I moved to the Bronx and attended high school there.

When I moved to the Bronx, I continued in the college bound program there. I was so happy to be around girls. Taft was co-ed. I smiled for six months straight. I played on the school's college bound basketball team for a little while. I was a very good basketball player. I was good with my hands as well. We played every day and often in after-school leagues. Boxing was to take charge shortly.

In school I found myself in a program while attending college bound at my high school. At Taft, I had small classes. There were no windows in the school. We were at a location called the Annex, which meant it was about a block away from the main school.

Our focus was on becoming college material. I was blessed. I had to do well in school or get a job. Failure was not an option. I worked during the summers and, when I could, in youth programs. I graduated from high school, the first member in my immediate family to do so. When I realized it was over, I was purchasing a senior ring.

I became a boxer. I had punched a friend of mine in the face for "butchering," as we used to call it. That is, he was fouling or checking while playing basketball recklessly. I hit him real hard. We didn't have any referees. He called me a foul name. I had to protect my reputation.

The next day I had a confrontation with this person at school. I thought I really didn't want to mess up my pants, but if I had to, I would.

He said to me, "You like to fight, right?"

I thought, *Well, here we go.*

He said, "Meet me after school."

I wasn't going to punk out. I did, and he took me down to the gym. I guess, as a favor, he took me down to the gym after a confrontation in school to get my butt whipped. I guess, in Jose's way, he might have been thinking it might happen there. That was not the case unfortunately. I think I hit him too hard. This started a new chapter in my life.

That's how I met my father image, Doug. People said that Doug had won a fight against Ali. They said Doug was an older fighter, and Ali was up and coming. That made the difference. Doug taught me how to use my hands very well, so well they thought I would make a good pro. Doug, as a former professional fighter, was exciting. He was from Black Harlem and a legend.

I had found a mentor in Doug. He was one of the top heavyweight contenders at one time. I was near the edge of greatness. There were some great men as I look back: Dr. Martin Luther King Jr., Malcolm X and several other revolutionaries, Nelson Mandela, James Brown, and Michael Jackson. I had followed my family mentor, my brother-in-law. I became a boxer, as he had done in Cleveland. I believe, at that time, I realize I was looking for a father image.

The gym was on 165th Street and Sherman Avenue in the Bronx. I earned several trophies for boxing there. My nephew and I were still in competition. He was getting giant basketball trophies. I couldn't let him get away with that. We were very competitive. My trainer became my father figure. He was a big, tall, strong-looking guy. He was a big, strong fella, the type you saw these callouses, cuts over his eyes all puffed up, when you looked at his eyes. He talked with a strong drawl. You could tell he had been in some wars.

What I liked most about my father image was his ability to joke. He was always joking. He would said things like, "Yeah, I hit that turkey so hard I made him fart."

I wanted to learn to protect myself at a high level.

An older man was in the gym most of the time. He was a disciplinarian. Although he was an older man, he was smart and tough. He would spar with us. He had a lot of tricks. He outweighed everybody. He would let you have hot tea in the summertime. He let you chew gum if you "spit" out the sweetness.

The old trainer would put on the gloves, sit on the second rope with his back against the top rope, and beg you to hit him. When you were tired and wore out, he would clock you upside your head. He would step on your feet and then hit you with a right-handed bomb. There was a lot of tricks. He would grab you by the gloves and put them under his arms so you couldn't get out. He would spin you around. He would talk stuff. He was an old trickster.

The older trainer was a historian on the fight game. He would tell us about the old fighters. He would clown in the ring. Then he would bang you.

Best of all, the gym took care of you. They would pick me up at home to do road work in Central Park once or twice around the reservoir. They wanted you to get enough sleep. They watched what you ate and showed genuine concern about your well-being.

The better the fight, the better the friend. Ironically the fighters formed new friendships. The crowd was the angry bunch. The people who came to see the fight were all pinned up with anger. Then they came and told you to start warming up. "You are on next."

You walk out there, and you go. I didn't know all these people were out here. You might see family members, and you go, "No way am I going to lose." The bell rings, and it is on. I guess I had ten or eleven official fights.

The real fight took place in the gym. They were the hardest there because you are working on your weaknesses. In the ring you have a couple rounds to figure out your opponent's weaknesses and exploit them. In the gym you have days to exploit a handicap.

Miguel, a Spanish fella, was my sparring partner in our gym. He was heavier than I was, and his idol was Rocky Marciano. Do

I have to say anything else? He could punch. That meant I had to move fast and put my punches together. That's all Miguel had to do, but who was going to tell him?

He sometimes asked me for advice, but I couldn't tell him everything. That was why we had the coach. One time Miguel hit me so hard that I was on my feet, but I thought I was in the locker room, putting on my boxing shoes. Of course he didn't know it. I didn't tell him that either. The wars were in the gym, not the ring.

Then there was Bob, who was fast, tall, and kinky. He went on to become a golden glove champion. He was in the weight class above me. He was between Eddie and me in weight. I became a puncher boxer for him. I almost knocked him out. I put my stuff together. We were one family and traveled as a team. The roughest fights were among us, preparing for something else. I had an opportunity to turn pro. I chose school.

Jazzy, our heavyweight, was a character. If you got to the third round, there was a chance he would tire out at the end of the second. He was questionable. He always seemed to run out of steam. Most of the big guys did in the later rounds.

We would fight out of town on the weekends in what we called "smokers." That was where we got the trophies. The father figure and the older man did the matching, and we did the fighting. It was like being a gladiator. I think they used to secretly bet on us.

I was never afraid when I got in the ring. It was time to go to work. Let's say I was nervously fit. The hardest time was waiting in the locker room, hearing the crowd roar and then listening to silences, like a gladiator in Rome maybe.

Being nervous and in great shape was an awesome combination. My left jab was like a machine gun and a pistol combined. When you were in the locker room, you saw someone come in all bloodied up. When you heard the bell ring, it was like it went all through you.

They would come in and tell you what bout you were on. Then they would tell you who you would fight. You like to let it stay just a name. You didn't like to talk to people. They might be your opponent. You needed a certain mind-set, and you didn't want to mess it up by making friends before the fight. You could become friends later.

Later in the gym's history, professionals emerged from it: Dave Moore and Alex Ramos. They are some notable pros that I know. It was good to know that I had been part of starting something great. I changed directions for a reason, but the spirit never left me.

After graduation from high school, the first in my family I might add, I asked my oldest sister to wake me up at seven o'clock one morning.

She asked me, "Where are you going so early?"

I said, "To college."

She said, "Boy, I don't have any money to send you to college."

I said, "I am on a work-study program. I'm heading for my first day of college at John Jay College of Criminal Justice."

That summer I found out that I would no longer have work-study to draw on. I would either have to work at night and go to school during the day or vice versa. I realize that some of the teenagers I idolized went to Viet Nam that summer. I was never going to see them again. If I were drafted, I wanted to be drafted into a branch of my choosing.

That summer while working for the Archdioceses Society Youth Program, I passed the test for the US Air Force. I was nineteen years old. I took a trip to Staten Island and tested. I passed.

My recruiter asked how soon I would be able to go.

I replied, "Immediately."

Within two weeks, I was a six-year enlistee into the all-volunteer service of the air force. I was not drafted. I was the first of the volunteer service.

I chose school and college instead of a boxing career. I had to do some internal thinking. I had to choose between some people I didn't want to disappoint and a chance to make some money using my head. I chose the latter.

My days as a warrior had just begun. This time I had skills. I could handle most people pound for pound. My heart was much bigger. I think, at that time, I learned to control fear. I learned to react under pressure and to perform at a high standard.

It was a chance to get a college education and work at the same time. I would have a career and get paid, even if I were to be a police officer. I would have two stripes after basic training. Lackland, Texas, here I come! Not many kids where I lived got the opportunity I was about to get. Inner-city kids all over the nation were enlisting to escape their circumstances.

I had a girlfriend, but I couldn't afford to shack up so I choose the military. Maybe I would come back and get her. She couldn't wait. Her mother was marrying for the second time. Her husband-to-be had a young son. I couldn't share my girl with anybody. I think she became desperate as many young girls do when they wanted to leave home.

I attended basic training in Texas. I think basic training was eight weeks at the time. Then I had two more weeks of technician school for security police. I would receive the rest of the training on the job at my next base. I just wanted to leave Texas. It had been traumatic.

Fifty of us unlucky souls bobbed up and down in a San Antonio auditorium as our assignments were read.

"Minot, Minot, Minot."

As everyone laughed, we braced ourselves for the unexpected. My girl was shacking up with someone. When I got back home, I knew it. Oh, well. It was a big world out there.

While stationed in North Dakota for eighteen months in the dead of winter, I learned to hate cold weather. I think there was one person out of my basic training class and two homies from New York that I knew from technical school.

Technical school was an extra two weeks after basic training for military police. I almost went into K-9, the dog training portion of the military police, except it would mean extra time on the base for training. I loved dogs, but there was the extra time, and then you had to clean up behind the dogs. I didn't like that part.

I would go to the Bronx for the last time in my life to call it home. This would be the last time where I felt that connection. Good-bye, New York. World, here I come. Off to North Dakota! We were the first of the volunteer service reporting for duty, super troops. Johnson was a buddy I had met in technical school. We both lived in the Bronx. We were on the same flight to Minot, North Dakota.

When we got to the base, our first duty station, we were given a choice. We were given temporary quarters while awaiting training. We would be separated into two different sections. We had special clearances to work around special weapons systems.

When we got to training, Johnson chose missile security duty. I choose aircraft security. Missile security went out for three days and were off for four days, that is, when the weather allowed them. I reasoned that I wanted to be kept busy working five days on and two off. There was nothing to do. I would be bored to death.

I liked the idea of guarding a nuclear-loaded B-52. "Two-man policies" was a term used to explain a security situation where two people had total responsibility for nuclear security. This was an awesome responsible for the security of the nation. If they got by you, national security was at stake. Wow! The instructors told me that the aircraft, a B-52 H model loaded with a nuclear weapons on alert, was mine. I got to station, and I believed them.

With the two-man concept, no one was allowed within ten feet of the system alone, not even the pilot. I was armed with an M-16, an automatic rifle, grenade launchers, a machine gun, and smoke. I was a part of a super troop, really a Strategic Air Command. I was a trained killer. This was a special unit, one of the best in the air force. My counterpart and I controlled entry to the aircraft. We could use deadly force. What about responsibility? I now had two stripes. Airmen First Class Lundy was my title.

We were highly disciplined airmen, and we had top secret clearance to boot. The other area in training after we got to Minot was intercontinental missile security. My friend begged me to take it. It was more time off. But I wanted to keep busy. This place was no joke. My friends said I was stupid and told me that they would catch me and outrank me. I had enlisted for six years. They had enlisted for four. I had two stripes out of basics. I think the year of college prior helped me. While in New York, I had finished a year of college while living in my sister's house. Maybe that was how I became a cop. They had recruited from the school.

My fellow airmen didn't realize I was accumulating time in grade. They never caught me. I think they envied me a little. They thought I had made a big mistake by signing up for six years. But I would need to be a super troop to pull this one off. They had forgotten about time in grade.

I knew it was going to be cold, but not like this. When we got off the bus from the airport at Minot, it was extremely cold. I had on the long overcoat with the long spit in the back. It slapped me in the face. Arctic temperatures was the name of the game here.

When we got to the chow hall, the dining facility, I couldn't stop shaking. We got two weeks of training, and off we went to the world of aircraft security. Nuclear-loaded aircraft first stopped the Soviet Union, the Cold War. It was forty degrees below zero with wind chill sometimes getting to seventy degrees below zero.

We were given a cold weather briefing, letting us know how to dress. We were to dress in layered clothing, Arctic-style. There were special shoes called bunny boots, flight pants, a quilted pair of pants, Arctic parka, long johns, and a mask to protect the face. A pair of Arctic mittens was not enough. None of it kept you from getting cold in that environment for long. We started to call that place "The Not," that is, the not-for-real.

A shift could be from eight to sixteen hours. A regular shift would be eight, but the weather could get so bad that they couldn't get out relieving us sometimes. I had been on post for over eighteen hours on base. We had bad storms and whiteouts, times when you couldn't see two feet in front of you, where your relief couldn't get out to get you. You couldn't drive because you couldn't see. Sometimes we had readiness exercises where they forgot you unintentionally.

I did not want any time off in this cold place with nothing to do. I wanted to work most days. I didn't care if you got three or four days off. I needed to keep busy here. There was nothing to do. I was to learn to forgive is not SAC policy. Only two or three of us out of the initial group that I knew of made it out of Minot successfully.

If you were lucky enough to be in a gate shack, normally a shack with a Coleman oil heater, it could not go above forty degrees. They didn't want you to sweat. Sweating would cause you to get frostbitten, which meant being written up. Frostbite is freezing of the flesh. Remember, the cold weather briefing told you how to dress in this harsh environment. The supervisors were covering their butts.

They would have to write you up for being unprepared. Frostbite can mean amputation. I have seen men's mustaches break off and fall on the ground. You would get ice particles in your mustache and rub it, and it could fall off. If you touch metal barehanded, it would burn you. It could happen in three minutes approximately in temperatures like those.

How long did I have to stay here? I would get so cold that it felt as if my bones were actually aching. We would wear Artic clothing, which consisted of specially padded or quilted pants (bunny pants). Then we would have an Arctic coat that could be zipped up where there was a hole as big as a baseball, which would be followed by a mask, which had room for seeing and breathing. We had Arctic gloves and an Arctic boot. This was documented with your signature for protection from litigation.

Off we went with a cold weather briefing that asked us to dress in layers. No matter what you wore, if you were out there, you would get cold after twelve or fourteen hours. There were times that we went to post and were not able to be retrieved at reasonable times because of whiteouts or others unable to drive out to get us.

There were these Arctic bunnies, as we called them. They were huge and somewhat like the large jackrabbits in Texas, but they were white. We marveled at how tough they were. We used to refer to all our Arctic equipment as bunny this and bunny that. Bunny boots. Bunny pants. And so on.

At times, we worked certain areas. We would use dogs if it got below a certain level. A dog's foot is not insulated under the bottom. We would have to pull the dogs and replace them with one of us.

This was not good for morale, especially when some of the supervisors were not sensitive to our needs because of personal bias. We were required to be given at least a five-minute break every half hour or less. Depending on your supervisor and the business at hand, this could be exaggerated. You needed God's help if your heater went out, your shack was defective, or you were placed in an area where there were no provisions.

We were talking about forty degrees below zero weather with wind chill. Believe me, the wind was there. Remember, we were securing nuclear components. We were considered expendable. Seventy degrees below zero with wind chill was not uncommon. It was brutal.

While stationed in North Dakota for eighteen months in the dead of winter, I learned to hate cold weather. I was trained for two more weeks as a security specialist. I was shipped to Minot, where I spent an additional two to four weeks of training for nuclear security and became a member of the 91st Security Police Group, working nuclear-loaded airplanes as an aircraft security specialist.

I was in the SAC. I later saw the dog handlers there in Minot. Even the dogs got to go in early, and we had to stay outside. The pads under the dog's feet get cold after a certain temperature, and they had to be pulled at Minot.

Often guys broke down and quit. Because of the clearance they processed, they were given a psychological evaluation, relieved of duty, and put on the goon squad, not necessarily in that order. There were problems at home for those lucky enough to have a spouse there.

Most of the personnel there were men. There were only a handful of women. I think at one point the count was as low as thirteen women and more than fifteen hundred security males alone. We didn't have women working with us. It was not allowed then in our career field. I saw friends suffer mental collapses.

I heard the wind hollering at a constant rate and being snowed in, not knowing if we could get to work and then not knowing if we could get off. Once you got out there, you didn't know if you were going to be fed or relived at the appointed time. Imagine if you had family there and you couldn't get to them. Let's say they lived off base. What a problem! No wonder there were so many young men between eighteen and twenty-five there.

This placed a special burden on African Americans males. No African American families were living there within at least a two hundred-mile radius. We would sometimes leave the base before it was shut down to try to reach Canada, which was about two hundred miles away, in subzero temperatures.

During the Cold War era of Nixon, Reagan, Carter, and George H. W. Bush, they had first strike capability during a nuclear holocaust to strike the Soviet Union. We were an elite force of sorts. We were constantly told we were expendable. That is, in a hostage situation involving these systems, you would not be considered in a hostage situation.

There were no trees in this area to stop the wind. They say a woman was behind every tree. If you could find one tree, that was the problem. For the first time, I realized there were Native Americans still living on reservations. I was a New Yorker who'd never heard of such a thing. This could happen on TV, not in the real world.

Sometimes when we had bad weather reports, we'd try to leave the base. We knew that long hours would be encountered if we got snowed in on the base. Those systems had to be protected. Maybe we could call in and say we were stranded.

Maybe we would make it to Canada for the weekend. Now I realize how stupid that was. That was stopped by telling folks they could not travel farther than a prescribed distance on their off times. Those were some tough times. I believe they shaped who I am today.

Most people received orders between eighteen and twenty-four months at Minot. However, there were people who had been there longer. There were people who had been there and gotten orders and then had them canceled for reasons sometimes unexplained.

You could lose your orders. Things could happen, which usually resulted in people going berserk. It was definitely a hellhole. Most people left there and were then sent over to Southeast Asia. And then guess what? After the tour was completed, they sent you right back to those northern tier assignments. Most people had identifiers attached to their manning position documents, and back you would go.

I personally served almost three years in Minot over a twenty-year period, my first and last assignment. I served almost seven years overseas. I managed to serve in upstate New York, Montana, Philippines, Texas for training, Honduras for short tours, Nevada, and Panama. I went to South Korea for four tours, each one at a different time in my personal growth. I had traveled in Japan and Canada. I was at different stages of maturity.

Ironically, exactly twenty years later, I was to spend my last assignment in the air force at Minot. I'll speak more on it later with the groin kick.

This technique I call the groin kick is highly effective because, like a kick in the groin, it will bring you to your knees. My students will have it in their books as technique number three in *Master Lundy's Hapkido*. This would be in their personal books. You can control how low or high your efforts will be when you deliver the technique. The receiver will never forget what happened.

I was supposed to go to Taiwan, but they changed my orders and sent me to South Korea. En route, I had additional training in Texas.

Johnson also thought he was going to Germany along with another New Yorker who made it out of Minot, another homie. New York had prepared us for the world. We went home then for thirty days and shipped to Texas, this time to Camp Bullis for air base ground defense training, especially for air force military police.

The groin kick was over, and I was about to enter into a new situation. The groin kick is a special one where one hand is placed across the body, not allowing the other to strike because it's in a position that will cause the second hand to become shorter and ineffective. We then step back, pulling the opponent forward with his palm facing the head. And then a groin kick is administered with the instep.

This next chapter in my life was another challenge. It was an extremely painful, challenging time. This was another plateful of events. The time I fought myself is even a better description of this experience. When you open a can, you perform a similar motion. Let's look at what might be inside. In the student's book, they would call this technique the "can opener" in our studies. This is how it relates to my life at the time.

After we had returned home following training in Texas, we were able to go home again unexpectedly because of the Fourth of July holiday and our training being cut a week. We arrived home, and my brother-in-law picked us up at the airport.

When we took Johnson home up in the South Bronx, en route to the west side, a heroin addict stood in the middle of the street and began to nod to the ground. We looked at each other and said, "We're home."

After thirty days at home, Johnson and I were off to Minot. The family remarked he hadn't changed. I had really!

Johnson went to Germany. I have yet to see him since. I was redirected to Kunsan, South Korea.

THE CAN OPENER

Technique #4

When I Fought Myself, Marriage vs. Career

A picture of me in uniform with a machine
gun (when I had to fight myself)

Unlike the groin kick, the experiences related to this situation were extremely stressful and required a strong moral attitude. They made you look for strength in areas that required an honest look at yourself.

The "can opener" was the title of the fourth technique in my system of training. Socially it reminded me of a time when I had to look within and evaluate myself. I had to fight myself.

For this technique, number four on our list, we used a spear hand block to start. Then you go under the opponent's arm, and in a can opener-type fashion, you step back and perform the technique. Again I hope my students will remember the technique very vividly.

When I think of what the experiences portrayed, I realize how strong their influences were in my life. They reminded me of how Hapkido played such a major role in my life. I had to analyze my moral fabric like never before. When I fought myself, who won?

Having arrived in South Korea for the first time, I must admit I was scared. I just knew the communists were waiting on me. One thing I knew without a doubt, I had to get out of North Dakota, even if it meant going overseas. I had never been overseas before. I admit it was a little scary. However, there are people in America who have never been to the city next to them. What a cultural change!

My friends told me that I would love it. They were right. I spent seven of my twenty-year enlistment overseas. Almost all of it was in South Korea. Once overseas, everyone becomes an American. We still had cliques, but we all knew when the stuff hit the fan. We were foreigners. We all pulled together.

I had managed to get an identifier that guaranteed me northern tier assignments because I was cleared to work around sensitive components. Sometimes it was not entirely by choice. I also had clearance.

I made it a point to go to the local personnel center in Minot at least once a week to put in a dream sheet, a request for an assignment. I was deployable worldwide. I just wanted to get out of Minot. We did that to keep our sanity. I saw men there develop serious psychological problems, mostly due to culture shock. I went to school, played a lot of basketball, and kept busy. The trips to the personnel office made you feel like you were trying to get out of there. The average stay was twelve to eighteen months.

When I got to South Korea, it was exciting. They were very cultural. South Korea was great considering what I had already experienced in North Dakota. South Korea was a lot better. South Korea was cold but was seasonably cold, not as frigid as North Dakota. There was more career opportunity there. People would count down the days. If you wanted a position, if you waited, you could have it. I matured as a young man there.

The barracks were better in North Dakota. South Korea had some mosquitoes that would wait for you outside your door. They were small in comparison to the ones in North Dakota, but they were vicious. Now that I look back, it was because of the rice paddies.

The odors inside and outside were strong. South Korea had some strange smells that would make you look under your feet. At that time they used human manure for fertilizer. The smell of kimchi and garlic were everywhere at every turn.

South Korea was exciting. They were culturally strong. South Korea had a three thousand-year history. They were a strong and hearty people. I had come of age. I was twenty-one or twenty-two years of age in my prime.

I could drink and party now. South Koreans had some great tailors. Clothes and shoes could be made cheaply. It was a chance to experience different cultures. It was no problem for a New Yorker. Lots of other people had problems adjusting, not so here.

This was my second station, and possibly one-third of my enlisted time was gone. I had plans. I would go to college in my off-duty time. I would work out using my boxing or basketball skills.

As a police officer, keeping in condition was a big part of my life. I used to play basketball every day at Minot. There was nothing else to do. However, there was not all that was planned for me. Here I had to use my time wisely. There was lots of things to see and do.

I had made buck sergeant, the first tier of the sergeant ranks, on the way over. I had three stripes. After eighteen months in service, I was Sergeant Lundy. They called me and others who were in the same boat as "six-year wonders." We were the first of the volunteer service. All had previous college credits.

We were the first of the volunteer service, and we were given incentives to enlist voluntarily. Prior to us, others were drafted into the military. This meant the government sent you a number, and by law, you were expected to serve in the military in a branch they chose. Lots of city dwellers went to Viet Nam. The teenagers of my day went one summer, and I never saw most of them again.

I played squadron basketball briefly while I was there. I met Preacher, and we became friends. He was a first-tier sergeant as well. He was not a six-year wonder. He had five years in. He had not enlisted for six years under the volunteer service program.

It was time to soldier. Preacher was a sergeant, also a buck sergeant, which meant the first tier in the sergeant category. At first I couldn't drive a jeep. We had a 151, a small utility jeep, used for patrolling. It had a stick shift. I think I burned out the clutch while learning to use the (h) pattern. Preacher helped me a lot.

I didn't know then that Preacher would have a great impact on my six-year enlistee life and my overall life. Preacher was the center and informal leader on the floor when we played basketball. He too was a product of the northern tier assignment. He was a young African American and a product of Grand Forks, South Dakota, the sister base of Minot and part of SAC.

Preacher was married to a South Korean national and had a family living off base. He was also a leader off the floor as well. He was one of our most mature sergeants and a role model for our flight at that time at work. Preacher was in his middle twenties.

This was his second tour after having been assigned in South Dakota with his family. He was about six-foot-three and very athletic.

Preacher was always in a joking mood. He was also a Christian. I don't remember if he were a minister or not. But he was very knowledgeable about the Bible. He loved to eat as well. The meeting would affect the rest of my life.

The South Korean experience would be a major turning point for the rest of my life. Kunsan and the people there at that time performed experiences that would, as I look back, transform my life.

The "wolf pack" was what we called members of the base. We were always on alert, and they would blow a horn to get us back to base. We frequently exercised for invasion. We worked harder and played hard.

I wanted to keep busy at Kunsan. I started attending classes on bases. I worked out by playing basketball. My plan was to do my time. I figured I would take another overseas tour and then finish my hitch and go home. My obligation would have been met, ending my military time and commitment to the air force. I wanted to finish college. That was not to happen.

The more I learned about South Korea, the more I was surprised. I was astonished to find how much the South Koreans had in common with African American culture. They had a deep respect for the elders. They were conservative in their clothes and loved to dress.

They were a proud people, and they could fight. They were a communal people who worked hard and stuck together. They called the women as "sister." They said it in Korean, as in black culture, even if they were not family. They called the men as "Adoshi," which meant "uncle." American blacks were in the middle of the civil rights movement in the States. We understood unity.

I saw family members in their actions, even though at first I could not speak the language. I saw grandmas who I had never known in my life, but I envision that's what my grandmother would act like. I saw aunts and uncles. I saw a people who liked to eat and drink. Nonverbal communication became highly visible. I learned there how important family position is to the communications process.

I later found out that the Japanese had enslaved the Korean people. They had suffered a similar experience like African Americans in America. They also were in a situation similar to the Civil War in American history. Their country had been split into northern and southern sections. Families had been split on both sides.

Nonverbal communications is what we learn first. I saw the people's character through their actions. We learned gestures and watched people before we approached them. They insisted that you call them mister, misses, and miss when you addressed them in their country, for example, Mr. Pak, Miss Young, and so forth. I liked that. They made you understand that you were the visitor. I started to feel at home in South Korea.

It was at the gym where I met Mr. Pak. When I got to South Korea, I was an athletic person. I went to the gym every day. I still had that boxing in me. When I wasn't playing basketball, I was studying Hapkido. I used to work on the speed bag, often trying to improve my timing skills.

Mr. Pak was a short South Korean fellow built like a spark plug. He was no more than five-foot-six, kind of a compact, little fellow. He had no hair in the front, the kingfish-type look. He was a very spry individual. I'd use my hands, and he'd use his feet. He always won.

He used to joke and spar with me. I had a good left jab. I found that his feet were longer. When I jabbed, he sidekicked. This Hapkido deserved a closer look. He told me that my hands were longer than my feet. In the gym in that one room, there was the Tae Kwon Do, Tang-Soo-do, judo, and Hapkido class.

The different martial arts classes had an imaginary line separating them all. You can imagine how competitive we were. We could all see each other. Believe me, we were in some kind of competition too. Everybody's class would try to outdo each other. Mr. Pak was really something. He used to flip people.

When I think of Mr. Pak, I think of a Jack Russell. He was fearless. I loved going to his class. I realized he was right. Maybe he knew something I didn't. I learned something new every day.

I had been a boxer and didn't believe too much in the arts, or karate as it was called. I relied on a good right hand. Until I met Mr. Pak, I did not respect karate or the martial arts that involved kicking. At the time in my culture, this kicking was considered dirty fighting. America, at one time, didn't respect a man kicking. Years later, after Bruce Lee made kicking popular, America took a special look. I started to view kicking as a midrange weapon.

I was fascinated at the new system of self-defense. I saw the grappling techniques as an effective close in systems. I saw joint-locking techniques as closed-in support techniques. I saw boxing as a complement, a Western style of combative artistry. Now I saw boxing as an upper-body combative art form in many systems of self-defense. Hapkido had it all.

I started looking around the corner into Mr. Pak's class, and every time I did, he was throwing someone with such ease. All I saw was someone's butt in the air. He was some kicker as well. That spinning heel kick was exceptional.

In one of the demonstrations, he would take an empty roll of toilet paper. We would put an apple on it, and he would hit it with a spinning heel kick and explode the apple. He was good with those handholds too. I joined his class. We were in competition with the other classes in the same room.

The Tae Kwon Do instructor was a thin fellow. Then the Tang-Soo-Do instructor was a middle-aged man named Mr. Lee. My roommate was in his class. The judo instructor was built like a weightlifter and taller than most South Koreans. And he was serious and methodical. Mr. Pak was frisky and fearless. He awarded me my first black belt. He was a great teacher.

South Korea had another secret. Beautiful women were there—feisty, bold, family-oriented, hardworking, and committed. I met Annie, my wife-to-be. During that time in South Korea, I saw some beautiful women. They were so ladylike. Yet they were very strong. I still believe that the women are secretly the backbone of that society. I think they really control things. That might be true in all societies.

Men, we must admit we can't do without them. They keep us from exterminating each other. Maybe it's their compassionate nature. South Korean people expect you to be a man. The women play their role as women and nurturer. Period.

South Korean women are homemakers who value the home. Don't get me wrong. They expect the male to be the major provider. They expect you to take care of the outside of the house and them, the inside in a partnership.

I liked the spirited South Korean women. They would get in your face in a minute. They were not afraid. Those women had these wooden shoes (clogs), and they would take them off and go upside your head in a minute. I saw it many times among themselves and others. South Korean women are short. They like spicy foods, and they are tough.

Us African Americans got a kick out of them. The South Korean women reminded us of the sisters back home. They respected their men and were loyal most of the time. They knew how to treat a man and expected you to act like a man. They expected a man to perform certain roles. They knew theirs and expected you to know yours. I respected and admired the South Korean culture.

Picture of the Korean International Hapkido Team;
Kunsan class headed by Mr. Pak at
Kunsan AFB in South Korea

Later I learned that Mr. Pak was from Seoul, the capital city in South Korea, and had been trained by the legendary Boo-Soo-Han. Grandmaster Han made the first Hapkido movie in the United States, *Billy Jack*. Americans were blown away. Until that point, it was considered to be dirty fighting for someone to kick you. This movie helped to turn America around. Mr. Pak taught me a lot.

Mr. Pak realized that most of us would not be there long in South Korea. At first he didn't teach a lot of handholds. He realized that most would only be there a year. It was better to concentrate on kicking rather than the more complex handhold system. I had six more months. I extended for an additional six months. He concentrated on the kicking.

Hapkido has some devastating kicking. I become some kicker, like him. My basketball skills made me a leaper too. I could jump very high. It can be used as a good midrange weapon. The South Koreans are world-class kickers. In Mr. Pak's class, there was even more. I had to make choices. I wanted to learn something new, and I wanted to use my basketball skills for my squadron team. Hapkido won over.

Hapkido, the art of coordinated force, would change me for the rest of my life. The South Korean experience would be a major turning point for the rest of my life. Kunsan AFB and the people there at that time performed experiences that would, as I look back, transform my life.

Grandmaster Kwang Sik Myung was a master Hapkido instructor who was a student of the legendary Ji Han Jae, the head of the Korean Hapkido Association at the time of my first-degree black belt certification. Although Mr. Pak Son Han was my instructor at Kunsan, Grandmaster Jae endorsed my paperwork for certification in 1976 in South Korea.

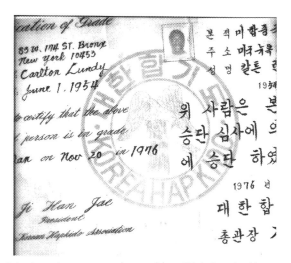

My 1st degree endorsed by GM Jae in Korea

The most famous of all the modern-day Hapkioist was once a presidential bodyguard for the president of South Korea. In South Korea, a grandmaster is licensed by the government and labeled the best in the country. Grandmaster Jae held that position. Grandmaster Myung was an author of four or five books on the technical aspects of Hapkido. (See the selective readings section.)

He was influenced perhaps by the father of Hapkido, who many say was influenced by a Japanese Aikido master. Hapkido is rooted in the grappling styles and has evolved over a period of time. I can't speak for what I didn't see, but in my lifetime, this is what I have learned about its history.

On my first degree paperwork, it was signed by Mr. Gi Han Han as the president of the Korean Hapkido Association in Seoul. Mr. Pak was my master instructor there, but it was endorsed by him. Mr. Pak later became president of the Korean Hapkido Association. These titles meant a lot to these men because they were licensed by the government. I lost track with Mr. Pak when he moved to Seoul on my third trip. The last time I saw him was in Osan, South Korea.

I have found many similarities with the Japanese Aikido system. However, the kicking system is totally and without a doubt South Korean. South Koreans are famous for their kicking ability. The elements of pressure points and the concept of concentrated power has evolved into modern-day Hapkido.

Traditional Korean martial arts has had an influence with the weapons application of the techniques. My experience was the "O brothers" in Kunsan, South Korea. I also was influenced by Master Kim in Daegu. This was a traditional and softer version of the grappling styles. It was called "KuK Sool Won" then. Today at Kunsan, it's called KuK Sool Hapkido. Any of us will agree Hapkido has evolved over the years.

Grandmaster Myung has done more to document the structure according to his teachings than anyone I know. Grandmaster Myung promoted me to third-, fourth-, and fifth-degree black belt holder. He has over two hundred schools under his federation and was located in thirty foreign countries at one time. Grandmaster Myung has been my mentor for more than twenty years. I attended seminars in Los Angles. Mr. Myung visited my class a couple times over the years at Langley. I have found him to be truly an honorable man. I visited him a couple times, the last time in 1999. I received my fifth degree from him.

Master Pak Son Han was my certifying instructor. I never met the legendary Boo Soo Han, Mr. Pak's instructor. Mr. Jae was legendary throughout South Korea. This was my experience with these legendary men of Hapkido.

I never met Mr. Gi personally, although he endorsed my paperwork under Mr. Pak in 1976. This was the time Mr. Myung published his first book, *Korean Hapkido*.

Picture of 1st degree Paper work for one of
my students at Langley A.F.B Virginia

Today the grappling systems have been called the martial arts of the nineties. The ultimate fighting systems have found the value of the submission techniques. They have become very popular. The system is not new. The application is.

They have taken the form of jujitsu. Aiki-jujitsu, Aikido, Hapkido, judo, and Chinese Chinna are considered the grapping styles by many. Most martial artists are disgusted with the way some of the ultimate fighting systems have developed. The art form or structure has suffered. Like Kool-Aid, too much water makes it weak.

I have always been a career learner. My Hapkido years were about to begin. South Korea, Japan, and China were some of the best places in the world to learn the combative arts. The Japanese Bushido code—or warrior code—made these countries strong in their combative skills. The Japanese culture definitely influenced both cultures. I have studied under four masters in South Korea at different times.

South Korea had one other secret. Somebody was leaving tracts, the Christian booklets that tell stories about getting to know the Lord Jesus Christ, all over the place. I saw them in the work area in the bathroom. In the barracks and the security vehicles, these little booklets were everywhere. They were all over the workplace and beyond. I later found that it was Preacher.

Preacher, looking back, was a saint. He led me to committing my life to Jesus Christ. I had been looking for religious answers for years, but which religion was best? Remember, I had grown up at a time of the Islamic movement in the United States, along with Dr. King. My family was Christian Baptist. I had not claimed it for myself yet. Preacher cornered me one day at the bus stop in South Korea, and I gave my life to Christ. That was just the beginning.

How could I explain leaving South Korea to my girlfriend (Annie) at the time when she didn't speak a lot of English? I didn't speak much Korean, almost none. A Korean English dictionary was the preferred instrument. I knew the way I was living was unacceptable. We had lived together downtown for over a year. She protected me and took care of me in her country in a hostile environment.

I wanted to please God. I must admit I wasn't going to church. At the time, the only people I knew who went regularly was Mr. Sheppard from Manhattan in my childhood. Mr. Sheppard was a strong father figure in my life. He was my childhood friend's father. He was known to take some drinks on Saturday night, but Sunday was church. This family was also from Virginia. God is awesome.

I was to later learn in life to not be so judgmental. Preacher had cornered me at the bus stop in South Korea, and I had given my life to Christ. Preacher was placing the tracts in strategic positions. I got caught. I can hear him now saying, "I got that rascal."

This was to be the most important incidents in my life to come. I learned to speak Korean. My wife-to-be at the time didn't speak too much English. I couldn't speak too much Korean. We had to make some big decisions quickly, my girlfriend and me.

We learned to speak from that dictionary. I still have it. We taught each other the language. When I was saved, I tried to explain what had happened. My girlfriend and her girlfriend laughed. They knew something had happened and I was all excited. That was the beginning of my Christian journey.

Until this point, I was a professional soldier in the military police supervisor. I was enjoying my hobby, the martial arts. Going to Mr. Pak's class every day was amazing. I was learning something new every day. But I got orders. How would I tell my girlfriend that I might have to leave her? Or would I?

I said, "I'm leaving."

And she said, "I'm going too."

I smiled and said, "No, you're not."

The fight of my life was about to begin, that is, when I fought myself. Off to the Philippines I went with Annie, my wife, in tow.

Annie was a real woman. She was dependable and no-nonsense. She was a hard worker. She used to make apple juice for me with a cheesecloth. We didn't have a juicer. As time went on, we went places together and had a good time with each other. She took care of me. I knew I had someone special. I fell in love with her. We loved each other. We started dating and lived together for about a year.

As a black man, I understood that America was not ready for interracial marriages at that time. We were fighting for equal rights in the States, the time of Malcolm X and Dr. Martin Luther King Jr.

I had asked the Lord for a wife prior to coming to Korea, but I didn't anticipate that it would be a foreigner. I had prayed after leaving the Dakotas. God had given me what I asked for. Was I man enough to stand up and do what I knew was right? If you are not a bigot, then how can you do this to yourself?

I thought of all the devices: *You can't marry this girl. You can't do that. You came here by yourself. Now leave by yourself. She doesn't speak English. You can't take her back to the States. You know that's what they want anyway. You're not a bigot. You grew up in a multicultural society, New York City. You know what discrimination is. You don't like it. How could you do it to someone else, you hypocrite? Lundy vs. Lundy, will you leave her? She has done nothing to you but give you all her love. What will her family think? What will your family think? What will America think? What will my friends think? You have six months to figure it out. Are you going to open this can? Who are you? Examine yourself. If your family doesn't accept her, she's your choice. You would handle the consequences. Are you for real?* For a young man, this was a difficult decision.

I was becoming a real man. Round one, are you a Christian? Round two, are you a hypocrite? Round three, are you prejudiced? If I weren't, I was going to have to make some real decisions soon.

I made the decision what I thought God wanted me to do. I decided I would tell my oldest sister that I was going to get married. If she couldn't accept it, well … She wrote me back and said she knew I was not a fool and to welcome her into the family. That was the best thing she could have said. I had made up my mind.

We married at Camp Casey in South Korea. We didn't have a formal ceremony. We got our visas the same day. Philippines, here we come. I had about two years left on my six-year enlistment. I had a plan. I regret to this day that we didn't have a formal ceremony in the States.

My wife had to give up a lot at the time, including her family and friends, to follow me. I realize now how much we really loved each other. Now I really understand and appreciate the importance of such things. We both were from similar backgrounds, and I believe we both wanted to be good parents at all cost. We were like two trout swimming upstream.

I reasoned I had eighteen months in the P.I. If the marriage didn't work out, I was still in the Asian theater. We would vacation in South Korea before heading toward the States.

In the P.I., they didn't have Hapkido. I just didn't have anyone who was a suitable instructor without travel, and I didn't approve of the traditional martial arts forms there. They had Arnis, Philippine stick fighting. That is not to say that Arnis stick fighting was not good.

Six months later, we got a place on Clark AFB. I played basketball on the squadron team. I entered one martial arts tournament on the base and was well received.

My sister and her husband visited us in the Philippines. At this time I hadn't been home in about three years. My sister said she was wondering if I were ever coming back. I will never forget when I picked them up at the airport in Manila. It was like a dream. They still talk about the trip until today. I had a 350 Chevy Nova. When I left home, I couldn't drive. Surprise!

When my brother-in-law got there, he was surprised. He said, "I see why you haven't been back."

We had a maid. Connie was Filipino, and she lived with us during the week. She helped my wife when she went shopping and was also there for companionship. I was living like a black prince. The Philippines was beautiful. If you weren't married when you went over, you were fortunate to leave still married. There was beautiful people and beautiful women.

I had earned a degree in industrial security in the Philippines from the Community College of the Air Force. I received an associate degree in administrative justice from Los Angeles Community College while there. I studied and received special qualification for a system that would put me in command and control of very sensitive weapons when I got to the States.

We stayed in the Philippines for eighteen months. When we left, we vacationed in South Korea for the last time before we headed for New York. When I made my fourth stripe, I attended a school for training that would send me to northern tier bases in the States. We stopped in Japan on our way to South Korea prior to going to the States.

Now as a staff sergeant, I would be in excellent condition to challenge my educational goals. Now I was armed with position, skills, and experience. Another chapter was materializing. 7Eleven was a convenience store here in the States that contains many items. My experience level at this time paralleled a convenience store.

CHAPTER 5

7ELEVEN

Technique #5

The Convenience Store, But Can the Family Take It, Parenting

My wife and friends Plattsburg NY
My wife, first row on the left

At the end of eighteen months, we went back to South Korea one last time on vacation before we went forward to my new assignment, Plattsburgh. I extended my enlistment to get the assignment and planned on going to Officer Training School (OTS) when I got back.

Annie chose to go forward to the States with me after two weeks of vacationing in South Korea again. I got to go back to see my old instructor, Mr. Pak. I practiced in the Hapkido class at Kunsan. It would be ten years before I would practice with him in a class setting again.

At this time I had taken on a lot. My plate was full. I was an opportunist, and I used every card in the deck. I had a family and now a wife, and for the first time, I was not the main disk. Annie and I had been married for four years. We had no children, but we longed for them.

I played basketball on the squadron team for the security police. In the Philippines, I played here and there with members of other styles in martial arts, but I was not satisfied. I got orders and was sent to Plattsburg AFB in upstate New York.

We were happy I was going back home. I had spent three years overseas. I was from New York City, but Plattsburg was a six-hour drive from the city although it was still in the state of New York. The city of Plattsburgh was thirty miles from the Canadian border.

Montreal was the Canadian city nearest us. In the Philippines, I had been trained on a new system for nuclear area protection. This was a secure inside position, but it meant permanent northern tier assignments for sure. I also had a chance to study. We had no children at first.

When I got to the States, I was in control of the area tactical response forces. As a result of the opportunity, I could study while on the job and in the crow's nest.

I had set myself up for my next move. To go bootstrap, the program allows staff sergeants in their junior year of college to be relieved of duty for a year to finish college. They then would be eligible to be commissioned as an officer. You were expected to pull yourself up by your bootstraps. I tried to become a first lieutenant in the air force.

To God be the glory. Our first child, Freda, was born at Plattsburgh AFB. I planned to get my wife her citizenship, finish college, and go to OTS. Most of it worked out.

While in the crow's nest, I was planning how to get to OTS. I was attending classes at Plattsburg State College. I needed ninety credit hours to get in the bootstrap program. I had them now.

How could I get the command to agree to let me be relieved of duty to attend college downtown at Plattsburg State University? The squadron found out that I had a security clearance. They needed a body. The crow's nest is a sought-after position. Now looking back, if I were gone, a new position would open. Bye. I had other plans anyway.

My wife was pregnant again, and they wanted me to go on a special assignment for four months prior to being accepted into the bootstrap program. I went and used the assignment for leverage. Our second child, Angie, was born two weeks before I left.

I managed to convince the commander why he should allow me to attend OTS. I made a convincing argument. There were some problems.

The name 7Eleven came as a result of the positions behind the back in technique number five. As we begin to squeeze the hands in an accordion fashion, we call it "seven eleven." My students will be most familiar with the technique. The other associations with this technique socially is that 7Eleven is a convenience store in most neighborhoods in America. You can buy most of what you want there. At this time in my life, I could obtain many avenues, but what would be the price for the purchase?

How could I get to OTS? In the last chapter, I fought myself. I now found that, over a period of time, I had developed numerous new skills. Like a convenience store, I have a variety of resources. I could become a commissioned officer in the USAF.

We finally had two children. I had made another stripe and was headed toward home, this time as a staff sergeant, the second supervisory tier in the military police.

The first day that the baby came home, I was scared. I have to admit I was a little jealous. But all fathers know that comes with the territory. I was determined to be a good father. My wife was an excellent mother. Also we came from weak family backgrounds. We were willing to succeed at all costs. We loved each other. The yearlong enlistment would be up soon. What was I going to do?

When my wife was pregnant, they wanted to send me to Nevada for four months. I didn't want to go. I took the assignment so I could get leverage to get in the bootstrap program. It was not an easy four months in Nevada. Thanks to friends and other South Korean nationals, my wife was able to manage.

I spent my time in Las Vegas on the weekends. You would be surprised to find it can be a very lonely place if you are not with the ones you love. I met some old friends from South Korea there. I spent time with them whenever I could. This was a long four months.

When I got back, I used the material from the assignment and my work in the area to help me get an endorsement from my supervisors. I was relieved of duty to go to the bootstrap program. I was assigned to temporary status as a full-time student at the local university.

Once I completed the degree requirements, I would have to apply to OTS, provided my grades were good enough. I received staff sergeant pay and got to live in base housing while I was in school.

I was a good provider. I was lacking, I think, in the loving husband part. I internalized pain. I'm a surviorist. I was pushing hard—new family, school, OTS, passports, citizenships, visas, and assignments. My wife was a tough cookie.

While I was in school, I received orders to return to South Korea. On top of that, I received two D grades, which lowered my grade point average (GPA) to 1.90. I needed a 2.0 to graduate. I had orders to Daegu, South Korea. Would I have time to finish school? Did I have time to get passports and visas? My youngest daughter was not born yet. My wife was close. Would the baby be born in time?

The tour was unaccompanied. Was there a way to get the family to South Korea? I could have my wife and children shipped because she was a South Korean national. At this time she was also a citizen of the United States.

My wife's citizenship was based on a test, and because she was married to a military member and traveled, it created less hardship. I would send them to stay with relatives in South Korea until I joined them. I had training en route. Thank you, Jesus.

We got the passports and visas. Angie was born two weeks before. I was able to get her passport and visa. Annie got her citizenship. South Korea, here we come. Thank you, Jesus.

I had to leave Plattsburgh without my diploma. I started getting D and D-plus in academic areas. I passed everything that year, but the Ds tore up my cumulative GPA. I gave everything my best shot, but I wanted to do the best for my young family. Was I pushing too hard? I was nearing the ten-year mark. If I were selected, I'd have ten years as an officer to retire as one. I only wanted to spend twenty years, but things were getting tight. Then I got orders. South Korea again. The news was bittersweet.

I was selected to go to college for a year in hopes of becoming an officer. The problems started to accelerate. I was in school while my wife was pregnant. Then I got orders back to South Korea. I ran into trouble with my college grades. My cumulative GPA was too low to graduate, even though I had not failed any course work. I could not apply to OTS from an overseas location. Also I needed passports and visas for my wife, child, and one who wasn't even born yet. How would we work it out?

A couple of good things happened. My second daughter was born, and I was able to get her an infant passport and visa, along with her sister. My wife got her citizenship. I had a chance to visit my wife's family again. Daegu, South Korea, here we come.

This second time, my family was with me. At least I was traveling with my new family. My GPA was a mess, but I didn't fail anything. This wasn't an easy task. There was a lot of praying in between. It didn't look good for getting into OTS, but all was not lost. I could take the classes over and bring up the GPA while I was overseas. I was a little beat up, but the family could take a break for a while. I had work to do.

I had training en route this time. I sent my family ahead of me, and off I went to Texas. I was going into a potential combat zone, and I needed additional training on air base ground defense. I would later join them in South Korea for the second time. Back to Kunsan, my old friends, Mr. Pak and Hapkido. I would make second-degree black belt this time.

These northern tier assignments were now common. The choices I had were Southeast Asia and the northern part of the United States. Could I get a break? I continued to take college classes while overseas. I took the D courses over and got Bs. I made second degree under Pak Son Han. It had been ten years between my first and second degree.

I had a friend in the army. He told me about Grandmaster Myung. I had orders to Malstrom, Montana. I was there for eleven months. I joined the Stinger missile program. I got orders in eleven months. I sent my family to South Korea. They joined me in Daegu, South Korea.

I met Master Kim and studied under him. He was a big man, but Daegu smooth and light on his feet. I was not promoted by him, but I was satisfied I found someone of his caliber. I didn't have enough time.

I spent my time at Daegu trying to improve my GPA. I also volunteered for a special program called Stinger. We had an American-style apartment off base in the city. My wife's mother came to visit us. Then came orders, this time to Montana. Montana, here we come.

The children were under five years of age. At Daegu AFB, it had a small American support detachment. I managed to get a car so I could commute back and forth to work. I was the flight chief (or boss) on the night shift for ten to twelve military police officers. I got the car because I had paperwork saying I was mission essential. I needed a way to commute from downtown, and I had a number of stripes by that time.

It was a nice American-style home with inside plumbing and modern appliances. It was better that what we had in the States. I managed to get an old Royal Record, a black South Korean compact car. All cars there at that time were black. I needed it to get to and from home. It was a South Korean hoopty.

My wife's mother came to visit us. It was a pleasure for my wife to have her there with her. When I think of it, I had placed a lot on my wife. I was very ambitious. Off we went to Montana. We realized the children would one day have to return to the States. They were bilingual now. They spoke Korean to their mom and English to me. We were not the only American families in the area.

Camp Walker was a large army base on the other side of town. It had a lot of Americans. I couldn't read Korean, but I used landmarks to drive through the city. It's funny how you don't have to have street signs to get where you want to go. I was navigating very well.

Could I find a master? I had a first-degree black belt. During this time, my martial arts technique was refined. I met Master Kim at K-2, the airbase. It was half Korean and half American air force.

At that time I was a black belt holder for approximately five years. Could I find suitable instruction until now? Mr. Kim was well-qualified and one of the best technicians of the arts I have ever known. He took me under his wing. I studied martial arts under him for about eight months. But I didn't receive my second degree.

Mr. Kim was a good karaoke singer. In Daegu, I found a good instructor. He was big but very agile. He made us tapes. I met Brown, then the highest-ranking brother that I knew. He was in second training for third degree. Between him and a black Ranger I knew in South Korea, they were the highest-ranking minorities I knew in the arts.

After an extension of my tour, I was headed to Montana, this time Malstrom. This was beautiful country, but it was not for me. We managed to get housing rather quickly there. It was cold, forty degrees below zero at times. We met a couple there who would be our friends for life. We stayed at Malstrom for eleven months. I got orders to return back to South Korea for the third time. This time, it was Kunsan again.

We left from Daegu to go to Montana. This would be our last time in South Korea with children. This time, the girls were under five years of age. We realized, the next time in the States, they would be school-age. We would have to think about settling down. The kids thought something was wrong with me because I couldn't speak Korean as well as they could. That was okay. I understood everything.

Prior to leaving Daegu, I had put in for a special program called Stinger. I didn't know it then, but I was accepted a couple months after I got to Montana. That's why my tour was so short. I found out shortly after I arrived in Montana.

You had to plug in your car to keep the engine block from freezing. You wanted to make sure you had a reliable vehicle. I was working in the alert area. No planes were there six days a week. There were no planes in Montana.

I worked as communications plotter in the nest alarm monitor for the area or response leader. I must admit I got bored quickly. Montana was beautiful, but it was not for me. We met some friends there who would later join us in South Korea for the third time. I had to keep going back to stay out of these northern tier assignments.

It was fifty degrees below zero in the winter. They used to say, if you don't like the weather in Montana, wait thirty minutes. It was true. The temperature could change forty degrees up or down quickly. I'd take South Korea.

We met the Carters there, who were to become lifelong friends. They were an interracial couple. The father was black, and the mother was South Korean. They had two children as well. Our children grew up together.

In Montana, I saw a real bear down near my fishing hole. I was ready to leave right then. I saw him from my car. I had too much city in me for all of that action. That was the end of my trout fishing days in Montana.

This is one of my dreams. Thank you, Jesus. I was traveling on the wind. I had become an opportunist. I had learned to become a survivor and use what resources I had. This might have been my greatest advisory. I was later to learn who was really behind my success.

I was at Kunsan for the second and third time in South Korea. I became an adjunct professor. I had managed to get another hoopty and live downtown with my family. I took the Hapkido class on base.

The base commander was in my Hapkido class. The squadron commander was head of the security police. The base commander was in charge of the base facilities. Mr. Pak was very happy. I remember him saying that I had given him a big face. It was his way of saying he was proud of me for rejoining him in Hapkido. He promoted me to second degree. The base commander being in our class was special.

A friend set me up. While reviewing my academic records in the education office, he convinced me to start teaching criminal justice classes. My reply was, "How?" I even managed to get a teaching job as an adjunct professor for Central Texas College teaching criminal justice.

At Kunsan I had become an adjunct professor. While taking extension courses on the base, I met the director of education at Kunsan at the time. He worked for Central Texas College as an administrator. He was a civilian contractor. He asked if I would like to teach criminal justice. He said he noticed that I had finished my degree. All I needed was an associate's degree to teach. I had one, a two-year degree in administrative justice from the University of Maryland.

He explained the criterion. He explained that this area overseas was a hard-to-fill area. Because I had more than five years in law enforcement, this was my career field I could teach in. A professor in the States would write the syllabus; I would read the book. I could administer three tests that the department in the States approved.

What if they asked me a question I couldn't answer? The administrator advised me, if it were not in the syllabus, they didn't need to know. I loved it. It was the easiest money I had ever made. I made six hundred per student.

Someone said in one of the courses, "My brother is an officer in L.A., and they do it this way."

I replied confidently, "The book wants us to do it this way."

I had a two-year degree in administrative justice. I could use the expertise from members I knew in the field for validity. I could do crime scenes and fingerprinting from military investigators.

I worked aircraft security now. My official title was security specialist. On a military installation, it is like being in a planned community. We were self-contained. I had a lot of experience protecting USAF resources of all types.

You would be surprised what a letter of recommendation from a college class can do for a military career. I used the many tools at my disposal. I used the hospital and law enforcement personnel for some areas I was least familiar with.

I paid them with letters of appreciation. For military people, this meant food for promotion. I solved any problems with validity. I used special investigators for technical knowledge I might encounter and was not proficient with. I used the book for the course for cover.

This was an extension of Central Texas College in the States. A college professor would write the syllabus in the States. I could also get my coworkers to select the courses they wanted to take and get them for them. My audience was fellow security force members of the wolf pack, as we were called. A major was the police commander.

I felt like an actor. Each class was like putting on a Broadway production. It was fun. I enjoyed the students appreciating learning. I used my peers on the job. The students loved my classes. I tried to get them the classes they wanted. I taught for four semesters.

My time as a teacher had begun. This was what I wanted to do after I got out of the military. OTS, you have met your match. I extended for six more months on my one-year tour in South Korea.

I now had a bachelor's degree in sociology with a minor in criminology. I taught my fellow security police officers police courses at the college level. Central Texas would send me the syllabus and the book.

Picture of The Korean Int'l Hapkido Team; Kunsan class headed by Master Pak – in Kunsan AFB South Korea

I would read the book and send them for tests relating to the materials. When the test was approved, I got paid. It was the easiest money I had ever made. 7Eleven. This was like a convenience store. This time I had skills.

Teaching school and Hapkido instruction was the plan for this time at Kunsan. I had a chance to reunite with Mr. Pak. This would probably be my last time in South Korea with the family. The children were becoming school-age.

I was to return to Mr. Pak one more time at Kunsan. He later became the president of the Korean Hapkido Association, no doubt a great honor for him. This was quite an honor in a country where so many masters had devoted their lives to Hapkido. I think that was one of the turning points in Mr. Pak's life.

I returned to South Korea and Mr. Pak to receive another degree. After returning over the years, I put the handholds together. I started to learn the advanced kicking and weaponry that were passive weapons: the short stick, middle staff, long stick, cane, and later ropes.

Mr. Pak had the base commander in that class. He said, "Lundy, he's the base commander. Don't kick him hard. Take it easy."

I respected the commander both as a superior and real leader. He was a very humble man.

As Stinger flight chief on the day shift and adjunct professor, my experiences were paying off. It was like a convenience store. Go in and get what you want. The commander at Kunsan was in our Hapkido class. This had special significance. He assembled a group for a demonstration on base of the best Hapkioist in all of South Korea. The base commander's status helped Mr. Pak to get the best Hapkido people in all of South Korea in one place for this demonstration.

Their Korean International Hapkido Team and the members of our class participated. I was the head student for our class at Kunsan. I realize how blessed we were to be in that space and time.

The commander at Kunsan later married a member of the international demonstration Hapkido team. I will always remember them. She was a young master at the time, a fourth-degree black belt. There were only two female members that I remember, and she held her own, believe me.

I realize now that Mr. Pak played a major part in my life. Other than family members over the years, he made the most lasting effect on my life. Now almost thirtysomething years later, I'm still feeling the effects. These were some honorable people. Wherever you are, if you read this, I am grateful, my Kunsan family.

That's where I met my good friend until this day. He studied Kuk Sul Won, also a form of the grappling styles that is very close to Hapkido. Perhaps they overlap in areas. Remember the authors are the same people. I believe they all shared technique.

The night shift Stinger flight chief was one of my best friends. He and I, with the help of others, built a program with nothing but a mission statement. We are now lifelong friends. We were drinking partners also. We loved Korean rice wine. We still keep in touch, even to this day. We shared martial arts material. Often the military offers you history-making opportunities, and this was one.

The major at Kunsan was later to be my squadron commander at Langley and recommended me for a special program there. This would help the hold program overall. I was an adjunct professor for Central Texas College, teaching criminal justice courses. My fellow airmen were selecting the courses, and I was teaching them. They were getting educated. I was making money. This was the easiest money I had ever made. I loved it. The students liked me, and I was appreciated. I was a teacher.

Then I was a military police officer with over ten years of experience in the field and an associate's degree in criminal justice. I had earned a degree in industrial security in the Philippines from the Community College of the Air Force. I received an associate's degree in administrative justice from Los Angeles Community College. I also had a bachelor of arts degree from Plattsburg State.

I managed to get another hoopty to live downtown with my family. I became a flight chief on the base for a special program in the Hapkido class on base. It was like a homecoming. I was a flight sergeant for a group of men on a special assignment. I had five stripes. I was mission essential. I needed a car to commute to and fro. Thank God.

My girls were not school-age at the time. We lived downtown, and they had friends their age. Our longtime friends, the Carters, from Montana joined us. They became our neighbors, and the children's friends accompanied them.

I worked in specific areas as an alarm monitor, also under Major Pak in my younger years. I was later to run across him again in my retirement years. He later became a magistrate in the court system in Newport News, Virginia.

Grandmaster Kwang Sik Myung, a master Hapkido instructor, was a student of the legendary Ji Han Jae. Grandmaster Jae was once the head of the Korea Hapkido Association, the most famous of all the modern-day Hapkioist. Grandmaster Ji Han Jae was once a presidential bodyguard for the president of South Korea. In South Korea, a grandmaster is licensed by the government and labeled the best in the country. Grandmaster Jae held that position. Mr. Pak and Grandmaster Myung were all presidents of the Korean Hapkido Association, a high honor.

He was influenced by perhaps the father of Hapkido, who many say was influenced by a Japanese Aikido master. Hapkido is rooted in the grappling styles and has evolved over a period of time. I can't speak for what I didn't see, but in my lifetime, this is what I have learned about its history.

On my first degree paperwork, it was signed by Mr. Jae as the president of the Korean Hapkido Association. Mr. Pak was my master instructor there, but it was endorsed by him. Mr. Pak later became president of the Korean Hapkido Association. These titles meant a lot to these men because they were licensed by the government. I lost track with Mr. Pak when he moved to Seoul on my third trip. The last time I saw him was in Osan, South Korea.

I have found many similarities with the Japanese Aikido system. However, the kicking system is totally and without a doubt Korean. South Koreans are famous for their kicking ability. The elements of pressure points and the concept of concentrated power has evolved into modern-day Hapkido.

Traditional Korean martial arts has had an influence with the weapons application of the techniques. My experience was with the "O brothers" in Kunsan. I also was influenced by Master Kim in Daegu. This was a traditional and softer version of the grappling styles. It was called "KuK Sool Won" then. Today at Kunsan, it's called KuK Sool Hapkido. Any of us will agree that Hapkido has evolved over the years.

Grandmaster Myung has done more to document the structure according to his teachings than anyone I know. Grandmaster Myung promoted me to third-, fourth-, and fifth-degree black belt holder. He has over two hundred schools under his federation and was located in thirty foreign countries at one time. May he rest in peace.

Grandmaster Myung has been my mentor for more than twenty years. I attended seminars in Los Angles. He visited my class a couple times over the years at Langley. I have found him to be truly an honorable man. I visited him a couple times, the last time in 1999. I received my fifth degree from him. He visited me twice here at Langley.

Grandmaster Jae, the father of them, signed my paperwork for first degree when he was the president of the World Hapkido Association in Seoul. I never met him face-to-face. I believe him to be the foremost authority on the evolving art of Hapkido. Mr. Jae appeared in one of Bruce Lee's last movies. The grappling styles were to become popular.

Master Pak Son Han was my certifying instructor. I never met the legendary Boo Soo Han, Mr. Pak's instructor. Mr. Jae was legendary throughout South Korea. This was my experience with these legendary men of Hapkido.

I got orders on the way to Langley AFB in Virginia this time. Mr. Myung had been recommended by a friend when I got back to the States. Could I find some Hapkido at Langley? From South Korea, I had learned many skills. I was now a college graduate and held a second-degree black belt. After a ten-year absence, I was able to reunite with Mr. Pak and study Hapkido. I returned home with a second degree.

I was coming back with my family. My children were becoming school-age, and I knew they couldn't continue to travel as we had been. I was a parent now, and I had to plan for the future. Langley AFB, here we come.

At Langley, it took a while to get housing on the base. We never got it. Instead we got an apartment. The kids started school. I asked my wife to be a stay-at-home mom until the children started school. Then I realized I had eight years to go.

As a police officer, my stay at Langley for the next eight years was highly unlikely. As military police I would eventually have to move again. This was my seventh assignment. I needed a Hapkido instructor now that I was a second degree with over ten years of experience. I needed a good one. Where would I look in the States?

In the next chapter, now I have many skills, and my Hapkido skills are at their prime. I am able to use the many experiences as a "walking cane." As a person, you would use a walking cane for support. I was able to use my experienced background to reach new levels.

The walking cane is a technique that my students might remember as when we used a reverse sweep to take down an opponent. With both knees together, we then use the wrist as a walking cane and at the same time add pressure to the elbow.

What I had learned became an advantage to me. Students started to return. I stopped advertising. I started to develop a legacy. I had students prior and present provide support. One of my students returned ten years later. This time he came back to finish the course and brought his five-year-old son with him. This was one of the youngest children I had attempted to teach.

Although the techniques were advanced, how could I not let them work together? After that, two more larger and older youth joined. They were younger than I was accustomed to, but to see this little one take a leadership role at such a young age and hold his own, I realized that Hapkido becomes a family unifier.

I taught the very young members lots of kicking and not the more advanced techniques because of their ages. The father completed the course, but until this day, he has not picked up his certification. I tried to locate him though messages and superiors. In this case, I believe he found something more important than the certification. The two of them had something that Dad could always teach. Neither of the younger ones completed the course at that time. Their families were assigned to different areas, and they moved.

Once I had my daughters in the class. It was a Saturday class, and I had some other youngsters in the class. I took them to the museum during class time. I didn't teach the young ones the handholds and locks under twelve years of age. It was my preference.

My friends begged me not to teach my girls Hapkido. They said they'd never get a boyfriend. They were too beautiful to get hung up on Hapkido. I never pressured them. They later played basketball and ran track. Today they still remember the time when I used to pick them and their friends up. Today my girls are grown. I'm glad I shared that time with them. They still talk about the time I had them in the class. In my experiences I can use now as a walking cane, I can use many situations to lean on through Hapkido.

CHAPTER 6

THE WALKING CANE

Technique #6

Parenting, Sports, Family Life, and Business

First two female students I promoted
to black belt at Langley AFB

I'd started a martial arts program at the old gym at Langley AFB in 1988. It was its first traditional Hapkido program. I started with the adults, which were military and family. As time went on, I started a children's martial arts program there. I wanted a children's program so I could spend more time with my daughters in addition to the adult program.

I had come to Langley in my twelfth year of service. I understood in the military police field at that time that it was highly unlikely that I would be able to stay at this base for eight years. I was in a military police unit. We were deployable worldwide.

For our first home, we moved from some apartments in Hampton, Virginia. We had a place to stay, no matter what. What a relief! Virginia has good schools and many military families in this five-city area. If I had to travel, I had the security of knowing my family had a roof over their heads. The kids had a pet, a golden retriever named Brady. We had a nice backyard. We had a home, a three-bedroom ranch house. Thank God. It was a home for my family if I had to travel unexpectedly. I knew I would get orders eventually. This was basically for times when I couldn't take the kids or wife.

We decided that my wife wouldn't work before the kids were school-age. When the kids became school-age, she would help me. She didn't have to work at all. This was so she could be socialized in case something happened to me. I would have to go by myself. My children were school-age, and my wife now worked. If I had to travel, they might not be able to travel with me. Holding a military family together is difficult. Thank God she was willing to assist me in this situation.

One little fellow, Tiger, kicked so well and strong that it scared me. His spinning heel kick was devastating. Good technique is good technique. My daughters and a neighborhood friend's child were in the class with us. I hope he teaches his son Hapkido. In later years when he was accepted to college, he came by my house, and I was so proud. He and his sister attended college. They have become model citizens.

When class used to be over, they were at my house. Their parents were late coming so I had to keep the kids until they came. I admit sometimes I felt like a babysitter and not a martial arts instructor. I felt that, being a parent, I also had to serve and support my family.

When I was in my midpoint at Langley, I was a professional soldier in my eighth year of service. I had been sent to Honduras for four months that year on a temporary assignment. I didn't want to go, but I had to. Langley was an active yard for worldwide deployment. My students again stepped up and held the class.

I hoped to have been selected as a program designer for a special assignment at Langley. This was wishful thinking. I had a short assignment to address. I had been sent to supervisor training in Florida that year, also for six weeks, to leadership school.

I was writing programs from the ground up for the air force. In the air force, we are always trying to improve ourselves for promotion. We were always seen as career airmen, looking for ways to improve our selves. This might appear odd for people who are not military. Career military understand and identify easily.

My students were running the classes at Langley in my absence. I had trained them to step up into leadership positions in my absence. They had proven themselves time and time again. I was very proud of them.

I was developing brand-new traditional Hapkido programs to accommodate a changing group of students. I'd truly developed into an innovator. My martial arts class, like the military, had been taught in my absence. The next person in line picked up the baton.

When I think of it, my girls and I believe all that attended that class went on to finish college. My girls have grown up as very independent. I trained innovators. I'm hoping for some grandchildren one day. My hopes are that they too will be innovators and independent people.

Time and destiny has transformed me from the "convenience store" mentality mentioned in chapter five. I'm now in a place where I rely on my past experiences for support, like a walking cane. I have learned to work independently.

The training I'd had in developing programs and overseeing various security matters meant I could choose my job this time. I could be a trainer or an administrator. At this time, I was well-versed in air base ground defenses tactics. In prior times, I'd worked as communications controller for the air force security forces. I also was the assistant flight chief for security forces. I believed, along with many others, that I would be a good candidate for this new position at Langley.

My students in my newly formed Hapkido class will remember technique number six as the walking cane. I'm an experienced martial artist now with years of experience, both foreign and domestic. I don't teach the children under twelve the handholds and locks. They learn fast, and it's not age-friendly. They are capable.

I had acquired new leadership skills professionally. As an instructor, formally I was stronger. I was selected at Langley for the special assignment. It was also a chance to remain at Langley for at least another year or more.

My mission was to design a program and enhance the unit's ability to survive and operate in a combat environment. Socially, this was a chance to use the walking cane, that is, my past experiences. They can be enhanced both administratively and training wise.

I love teaching. It's a challenge. I was in charge of all security matters. My job was to train the whole unit. The 74th Tactical Control squadron was the command. I was the only security police officer there. I would now be in charge of certifying seventy or more people and keeping them certified. Weapons qualifications was a necessity. Some of my previous training almost got me shipped out ahead of time. The construction of the Stinger program from scratch in South Korea helped in my selection.

After eighteen months, I had a model program. I received plaques for weapons safety from a two-star general for a program I developed. My unit was being cited as one of the best in the command. Was that good?

The first Gulf War broke out. The first 117 stealth bombers left from Langley. Half of my former unit left. This special assignment had given us a warning order. This meant we could be deployed at any time. The war caused the command to look at the qualifications of these units. My unit was discovered to have more people weapons-certified than any other unit in the command. How was that?

I'd been offered another job at the command level. I had to send my entire program forward for review. I was offered a new job. I must say I came close very close to being sent to Iraq.

My bags were packed in my living room for that call at "o-dark-thirty." That's military talk for "at any time." I was in my eighteenth year of service. I didn't deploy, but I could have at any time.

The war was over! Yes, I was scared. I'd worked hard here. My mission was accomplished.

Do you stay where you go or transfer? I think I did things a little too well. How did we do? I had to send my entire program forward for review. I was offered a command slot. Would I take it?

My section officer was in charge of the mobility section, and he made it known. I got the command unit plaque presented by the general for weapons safety. My boss at the time took most of the credit. I selected a replacement for myself, the best I could find. If I took the assignment, there was a decision to be made. I chose from my old unit. I had developed a great respect for my peers and fellow servicemen in my previous and present unit.

I did have a family. Did I have time for one more adventure? There was a chance that I might not be able to come back to my family. I could get an assignment someplace else. That's material for another story. I put in for orders.

I got South Korea for the fourth and final time. The kids had a home, wife, and me. We needed a break. I guess I was getting to be too much. Maybe a little time apart would be good for all of us. I got orders.

I was getting "short." That's military talk for a little time left before you depart to a new assignment. Could I go on one more adventure before I retired? My feet were getting itchy. I had orders, Kunsan, for the third—and last—time.

I had the house. I was in my eighteenth year of service in the air force. A year in South Korea would mean my nineteenth. There was a possibility that I wouldn't get a follow-on back to Langley. I was hoping the air force would try to save money and return me to my family's location. It was a chance I would have to take.

I just knew they would send me back to Langley for the final year. It would save them money. I was in my late thirties. This time I would spend another year away from home. I thought it was going to be at Langley the last year. That wasn't going to happen!

After six months in South Korea at my new job as unit security manager, I found out that I had an assignment after South Korea to Minot. I was devastated. It was confirmed. My family would not accompany me. I couldn't blame them. I was not going back to Langley where the family was. That was what I thought. That was not the case. My family was staying in our own house in Virginia.

I had two years left in service before I could retire at twenty. This time I had another identifier. I was a Stinger flight chief from duty in South Korea. I had just come off a special assignment at Langley. I had proven I could work independently.

Having experience working with a tactical control outfit had sharpened my base defense skills. My air base ground defense skills were great. I landed a job in the pass and registration section at

Kunsan. For the first time, I had an administrative position. Or did I?

This time in South Korea was my fourth time. Now my third time at Kunsan, I had a serious background. I was a senior noncommissioned officer. I was a fourth-degree black belt now. My old instructor, Mr. Pak, ten years later, was not at Kunsan anymore.

Mr. Pak, my first instructor, was the head of the Korean Hapkido Association in Seoul. He was now in Osan, South Korea. Master "O" Rok Mann was the instructor at Kunsan. He taught Hapkido. I joined with him. I had a chance to study Hapkido under Master "O" Rok Mann from Kunsan.

I had a line number for master sergeant. After six stripes, it was time for administration work. I was tired of foxholes. I had been given a special assignment. In this unit I was a security manager, thanks to Sergeant Jason, my section supervisor.

It was my first real administration job in a military police unit officially. There was one exception. During exercises I had to be part of the exercise element. I drew up the weapons defense plans for the base. I went out with a compass and set up the sectors of fire. They were used as a base defense plan, proving I knew my stuff. The commander approved them.

I had experience with setting up sectors of fire with weapons systems. When I was assigned to the tactical unit in Virginia, I sharpened my skills. During exercises I would be in charge of responding to simulated attacks on the base. My previous assignment carried with me. I could only be administrative some of the time.

The reserve force leader and other team leaders were the quick response teams for base defense. We had base defense exercises, often at the wolf pack. At thirty-eight, this was getting old. You have to be in that situation to understand how hard it is. I could retire after this hitch. My wife and family were staying in Virginia, where we owned a house. My family had three cars at home. I didn't have a car and lived in the barracks. It was extremely cold.

Minot can be a depressing place without family. I didn't have family with me. The weather situation made the place worse. Not having a car was a problem too. I would not be there long enough to justify buying one. I had to make the best out of a difficult situation. It was too cold to walk most places. We could get snowed in at work. With survival kits, whiteouts could be a problem. I started a traditional Hapkido class at Minot.

If it weren't for my church family, martial arts classes, and some good friends, it would have been unbearable. Thank God I was able to win the approval of my troops and retire with dignity. Thank God for my family trying to support themselves in my absence.

I could have stayed longer and possibly made another stripe. I could have went for more stripes. I had the résumé for the last two sergeant tiers. I had to admit I was tired. My girls were teenagers.

I could go for OTS, but I'd need ten years to retire to hold the officer rank. I had teenage girls. It was time to let it go. I wanted out! Freezing was only part of the reason. Family had suffered enough.

I would retire from the air force after Minot. My family was not present, but my pastor was. I had a martial arts class there also. Some of the members were present from the class. God bless you, guys, wherever you are. To all of the Hapkido family, hello.

They gave me a plaque that had "one time finished" on it. It was in remembrance of my South Korean instructor, Master Pak Son Han, from Kunsan. I promoted three out of that bunch to first degree under the World Hapkido Federation endorsed by Grandmaster Myung. That was a very nice gesture. The honor guard gave me a special send-off. A twenty-year journey was completed, and I was off to Langley in retirement.

Finally it was back to family. I was gone for a total of two years with sixty days in between with my family. This was rough. The girls had grown. They were more independent. I was bringing changes to the household. It was difficult. There was stress on the marriage.

Two weeks after being home, I was offered a job as a deputy sheriff. I wanted at least two months to rest, but that's not the way it happened. The Hampton Sheriff's Department hired me. In small towns, the sheriff and police departments are one. The sheriff has more power than the police chief does. The sheriff is a constitutional officer elected by the people. The city council elects the police chief.

The police in this area made more money. They also worked less hours. I was recruited. It was interesting politics. I wonder how many people are aware of the politics. Policing has become very political. It is really a calling, I think, and not an occupation for these reasons of low pay and a servant's attitude.

I had been prepared for leadership roles in the military, formal and informal. Of the forty-five cadets in the academy, forty-three graduated. Two didn't. One decided being a policeman wasn't for him. The other's wife didn't agree with him. It was not because of academics or failure. I'm not saying I was totally responsible for their success, but I was part of a group effort.

Corrections and the sheriff's department handles court procedures, jailer activities, and civil processing. The police handles law enforcement. I became a certified patrol officer in law enforcement. I had to resign from the sheriff's department to go to the law enforcement academy. They hired me before I went to the academy. Failure in the academy was not an option.

Majoring in sociology and criminology gave me a strong academic background in criminal justice. While serving in the military on active duty, I taught it. These marks helped me to get a good position in the regional academy. I was president of my class.

Corrections and law enforcement gave me a well-rounded perspective on the social problem in society—academically, economically, and politically. I found that I couldn't help many of the inmates. They were illiterate. Some were adults reading at a third-grade level. I remember a note I received from a twenty-six-year-old for "toth pace." This was sad. He wanted some toothpaste. This guy was twenty-six years old in America.

I previously was blessed to become the president of my class during training while attending the police academy. The most difficult time was the first two weeks. It was the firearms certifications and the block on the law. In either one of these areas, you could get relieved easily. I was chosen during these times because of my military experience. In a competitive academic situations, it aided in getting us through. We set up studying groups to help each other and graduated forty people.

After I graduated from the Hampton Roads Regional Academy for Law Enforcement this time, it was my second time. I had also attended it for corrections academy when I was a deputy.

The difference was that the police academy was two weeks longer. The correctional academy included cell searches, civil processing, and court duties. I landed a job with the Virginia Port Police as a patrol officer.

In the correctional system, my martial arts skills helped. I was able to get on special teams, the SERT, as a deputy sheriff. This was the special emergency response team for the jail. I gained respect from the inmates.

I was welcomed in certain areas of the jail and not others because I was trusted. Of course we could go to any section. Some were more hostile than others were. It's funny. Even in tough surroundings, a man is only as good as his word. There is honor among thieves. Right is right, and wrong is wrong everywhere.

Maybe I should try another way. I loved teaching. They were asking for former soldiers to enter the Troops to Teachers Program. In the late 1980s, I began training in my off-duty time as a schoolteacher in the local school system. I attended Old Dominion University's Troops to Teachers Program.

This was a highly successful program. I wanted to help the youth, not only in the martial arts classroom but academically. I found many inmates were illiterate. Maybe if they were caught early, that might be most effective. Well, this was my rationale.

In the criminal justice system in this area, they had a very high turnover rate. It was not like the military where, when you go to be promoted, you could leave town. It was highly likely you had to leave town to get one. This is just my opinion. Military members were considered double-dippers. This had its advantages and disadvantages. This area has highly qualified workers but few positions for highly educated and skilled workers.

I truly wanted to be a little more helpful. Could I be more of a helper to the community? Eighteen months later, I landed a job with the Virginia Port Authority as a patrol officer. I was to be there for five years.

I gave the class speech at the graduation ceremony on behalf of our class, thanks to the help of a fishing partner, a colonel in the US Army. His foresight and experience helped me to deliver a worthy speech. I will be forever grateful.

I later landed a position with the Virginia Port Police to become a port police officer. There I learned about the trucking industry and ships, along with longshoremen. I learned the terminology of the industrial environment. I learned the difference between port and starboard. This didn't have much to do with airplanes. This was industrial and shipping terminology.

The port authority required a knowledge on terminology. This was a major issue because it saved time. A regular police officer not knowing the terminology and not being familiar with port procedure could tie up personnel with litigation and operations.

Large ships have to pay for the time they are loading. It's like they are on a meter. This was an opportunity to be employed by the state. My days as a port police officer had begun. At nighttime, I was a Langley Hapkido instructor and part-time college student. The port authority offered a state retirement.

It was an opportunity to better myself. I could also go to school at night, and we had earned many educational opportunities while in the military. We handled situations that involved hazardous chemicals and toxic situations. I leaned on past previous experiences.

I became a desk sergeant, and my military experience as a tactical controller or communications plotter came in handy. I was still a little thirsty. I had some extra time. Why not use my military educational benefits? I'd always wanted to teach. Why not?

I was an instructor, teacher, academic, and martial artist. I was a veteran, police officer, patrol officer, port police officer, and deputy sheriff. Looking back, the area I was least qualified on was being a good husband.

I was a hard charger. The urge to be successful has always become an issue. Maybe it's coming from all my experiences in life. My wife was a good woman. She stuck by me and was content to let me handle the family situations outside the home. But I was not prepared to handle a women of her caliber. I think of all the years she traveled with me and raised our kids. She learned my language and followed me with all of my ambition.

I retired in 1993. I was to divorce in 2001. Annie passed in 2003 of stomach cancer. Our lives changed forever.

CHAPTER 7

ABOUT-FACE

Technique #7

Goodbye Air Force Military Police
Squardron (My retirement ceremony)

This next situation turned me completely around. It was a turning point in my growth as an instructor. This chapter is called "About-face." I was now learning to fight. This type of fighting requires weapons to fight a spiritual battle.

At the funeral I realized my daughters had become young women in the way they handled the burial details. I was there to assist, but basically it was their show. I realized they had come of age.

I'm very proud of my daughters. I'm also grateful for the twenty-two married years God had given Annie and me. May she rest in peace. Sun Yong Lundy was the love of my life. We had separated and were living in different homes after the twenty-two-year mark. Angie, my youngest daughter, stayed with her. Freda, my oldest daughter, had gotten a full scholarship to Norfolk State University. Angie had gotten a partial scholarship to the College of the Arts in Philadelphia. I stayed in our first home.

I was so proud, and so was her mother for the both of them. When we took Angie to college in Philly, when we left her and departed the school, we drove off in two different cars. My wife and oldest daughter were in one; I was in the other. It was a long ride back to Hampton, Virginia.

Freda was with her mom in her last days. My youngest daughter followed my footsteps and entered the air force. She got a humanitarian reassignment to be near her mother in her last days. Angie was working in the Pentagon when the planes hit. Thank God she was off that day. I'm very proud of them. I love them very much.

Working takes my mind off some of the issues and life itself. I started substituting in the public school system. Which area do you want to teach in? Substitute teaching, here I come.

As a substitute, I think I found I loved teaching the elementary school level. I was still a police officer, but substituting in the school system is flexible. I needed work to substitute for the pain. I also loved children. I think I am still a child at heart.

At one time I had five jobs and no money. It was hard trying to manage a home, divorce, school, and everything else. Multitasking can be mind-blowing when you are operating by yourself.

The girls finally convinced me to sell the ranch house after their mother's passing. I lived there for five years alone. I had become a workaholic. So I moved into a condominium.

I took college courses online. I was in the Troops to Teachers Program at Old Dominion University. I worked as a police officer at night. Sometimes I substituted in the mornings after work. I can still remember my elementary school teacher. I later found out that my grandmother taught other people to read and write. She was the teacher of her day. When she died, my elder sister said I was in her arms. I don't know what it means, but I love to teach. I love children.

I realize I was destined to be a student. I became a career learner. I took courses online. Old Dominion University was a leader in online learning with courses teleported from a remote site. They called it telecom. Some of the classes were in the classroom with the instructor at a remote location. We could see him or her and interact remotely.

Anyway I could obtain knowledge, I tried it. I was in a program for K-8 grades, favoring science. I finished their academic program but was unsuccessful in passing the licensing test for the state of Virginia. After numerous tries and preparatory programs, I tried something different. I was able to teach all subjects as a substitute on a provisional license.

I lost a couple credits, but I used my veterans' benefits to enroll in a master's degree in education at Strayer University. I completed it with all requirements. I can now teach teachers. I have over eighteen credit hours at the graduate level. I can become an adjunct in education in most colleges if given the opportunity.

One day I looked outside of my window, and I saw every car in the lot gone except for mine. I realized how blessed I was. I was getting paid for working at home by the government. What a blessing. It's not about me. It's about Jesus.

I had a medical condition that would require surgery. I lived alone. I was in school. How would I handle it? My daughters lived in the D.C. area now. I chose to recover after surgery at my older sister's house. Half the problem was solved. I was a veteran now. I couldn't wait to get back to my place and resume my life. The girls came and got me, and I headed back to my place in Hampton, the condo. I appreciated my sister and her husband for their hospitality. God was not through with me yet!

I had to call on God while I was healing and recovering from surgery. I had become a regularly going church member. I was returning from a trip, of which I met a spiritual warrior. This person inspired me greatly.

A friend of mine once gave me some scripture too. This time I had to dig deep to understand that this was beyond where I was used to going. I turned to God, as I do whenever I'm on unfamiliar ground. I started to believe in my heart that he would bring me through.

There was Kunsan and Minot for the second time. I was away from home for two years. I was retired. Yes, I had religion. My divorce and the death of my wife weighed heavy on my immediate family and me. There was my recovery from my surgery. It was time to sing and give praise to the Almighty.

Finally the death of my best friend, my nephew, was tough. We were like brothers from early childhood. It seemed the people closest to me in the world had passed. My competition, my friend, my back, the one who understood me more than anyone else, was gone. My mother died early. My wife and now my best friend were all gone. Now what?

About-face! Most military people understand what this means. An about-face requires that you do a three hundred and sixty-degree turn. That means you go full circle. Socially I had reached a point in my life where the martial arts had taken on a new meaning. My perspective of Hapkido was turned around. My spiritual life was changed. It started long ago, but I didn't recognize it at first.

My first week home as a civilian, I attended church. On that Sunday at the base chapel, I gave testimony about how glad I was that God had brought me home after two years of exile and how he had given me twenty years of military service. That Sunday, a man I didn't know offered me a job in the Hampton Sheriff's Department. I accepted, and my career as a deputy sheriff began. I thought I would at least have a month off.

At the time I was thinking about joining the Bureau of Alcohol, Tobacco, Firearms and Explosives (ATF). It was a government service. My résumé fit it directly. The money was good. The only problem was it would require me to travel. Enough. Family comes first. That was my best option at the time. This was a timely offer.

Hapkido now has become a platform for me spiritually. I see all young people as family. All of the family is in need of loving consideration and attention. Every woman who takes the class, I consider this could be a person crying out for help. Every youth is a special case. How can I help? For every family, how can I help? My previous experiences with death have changed me.

My role as a martial artist, father, friend, confidante, teacher, and counselor has increased. Hapkido is no longer a business. It's not a hobby. Hapkido has become something more. It's a calling, a platform to tell the world there is a better way. Most are attracted to Hapkido because of the effectiveness of its techniques. After a few months, awesome confidence is experienced. I've found I can transform lives.

I started out working in the Hampton city jail as a deputy sheriff. I still had my business at Langley as a martial arts instructor. My students had kept it going while I was away. Bless their hearts.

In the jail, Hapkido can be very beneficial, as an experienced person can use it under control. You can get compliance without seriously hurting anyone or drawing blood. AIDS is real in that type of setting. If you can get compliance without shedding blood, excellent.

I later got on the tactical control team in the jail. I belonged to SERT in times of emergencies. They later sent me to the correctional academy where I became a certified correctional officer. My martial arts background gave me a unique advantage on the team. I was, by that time, a fourth-degree black belt holder. My martial arts background became evident.

We could secure situations easily without shedding blood. Remember, some people in the jail have the AIDS virus. The grappling techniques are highly effective. Hapkido techniques are very effective and warrant compliance. The officers are not told who has the virus because they might discriminate.

I attended the Hampton Roads Regional Academy, which consisted of officer candidates from five or six local cities along with park rangers and campus police. Policing can take many forms. Eighteen months later, I landed a job with the Hampton City Police Department. It is a five-city area where I live. Corrections and police academies are separate organizations.

Law enforcement paid more, so I could learn more. I would have more time to do as I pleased. I was still taking college classes at Langley. It was difficult. In an attempt to constantly better myself, I was selected from among fifteen hundred applicants for the Hampton Roads Regional Police Academy. Ten of us was hired for the city police. I was one of them.

In Hampton, as in our neighboring cities, the sheriff and police departments are two separate organizations. In some cities, the differences are greater. The police play a more dominant role in law enforcement. In cities, the correctional officers play a greater role in civil processing in the courts and transporting prisoners.

I realize that God had used Hapkido as my platform. It was a setup. This was extremely serious business. I was not to forget it. Chapter 6 was titled "Walking Cane." My prior experiences led me to a business and a hobby, definitely into something I never expected. I had lots of help before, but this was something else.

In the seventh chapter, I experience spirituality on a level I have never experienced before. I began to realize that it wasn't me behind the wheel. I learned I should go for the ride and not try to drive. Every time I try, I have setbacks. Let God handle it!

Chapter 8 is the hip throw. This is a time of letting go. It's not all about you. What a good time. The eighth chapter, the hip throw, is a chapter of uncertainty. Sometimes we have to travel on faith. This chapter and this technique requires you to fall forward, uncertain of your landing. The previous chapter, "About-face," is the transition, one way of thinking to look at things from a totally different view. Can I help you to accomplish extraordinary feats? Come with me.

CHAPTER 8

HIP THROW

Technique #8

Where Will I Land?
The Prom and Life's Lessons

Picture of my most recent batch of cookies with
the Major's family: Myron, Kyra, and Matthew.
I pray they never forget the experience.

I learned that Hapkido could be a powerful tool to learn life's lessons. Many people started coming from various places everywhere. I was not advertising. People were showing up by word of mouth. For ten years, people were coming to my class. My business was growing.

Minot Class in North Dakota

I enjoyed teaching different sets of people. I was initially concerned with only youth. Young airmen and then marines, sailors, and all branches of the military and their dependents appeared. Then it went to young families, husband and wives. Families were starting to show up. Fathers and sons were next. New families were being made. Then my first couple was married after meeting in the class. Then children of former students started to show up.

I once gave one married couple a hundred dollars to complete the course. I realized that, after more than ten years of teaching, I had not brought through a husband-and-wife team. They were my first. They now have a child. I can see Hapkido written all over him.

I too would no longer look at my role as an instructor as just another position. I had matured as an instructor and realized that my ability to touch and inspire people, old and young, was of the utmost importance. This was more than money. My task had become to make sure my Hapkido was enjoyable. I wanted the students to enjoy the class. I was not there to be a disciplinarian only. I was there to share a piece of cultural artistry.

I made sure the students knew they could stop at any time they wanted. My role was teacher, father figure, mentor, friend, comforter, and military confidante, whatever it took. I wanted them to know they could quit at anytime it were okay if their hearts weren't in it. Hapkido is not the most important thing in the world. To God is the glory.

This father-and-son team were students in my class. The father was extremely strong and large, and the son was lanky, tall, and fragile in appearance. The son was a middle child and had a sister who was younger and quite domineering for a while.

This young man was fascinated. He recognized, by not being physically stronger than most people, Hapkido doesn't rely on strength alone. He finished the course for a first-degree black belt. Malik, wherever you are, I'm proud of you. Your parents are too.

I noticed something was happening. Families were appearing with their children, including single parents and their children. I realized this was a good place for parents and children to enjoy together.

My health started to deteriorate. I had never been seriously sick my whole life. I needed surgery for a bad hip. Minot, that cold weather, had finally caught up with me. Age gets us all. I needed surgery. After my surgery, I recognized healing developed from the inside out.

I learned the value of healing spiritually before the physical. I went to Manpower, a conference headed by Bishop T. D. Jakes.

It lifted me spiritually up off the ground. I was to attend several more conferences in other states before I was assured I had my marching orders.

I went on a trip afterwards, of which I mentioned above. I didn't want a normal church experience on Sunday. I needed a worship experience. I went to a conference with some of the leading ministers of our time. After you have jumped, shouted, and rolled on the floor a couple times, then what?

My students stood by me during my medical recovery period. They had given me a conference call at my older sister's house, where I was recovering from surgery. I was so happy they were carrying on the class and advised me to hurry back.

They took over the class, as I had trained them. The class proceeded as normal. Having been in the military taught me to plan for others to take your place with their encouragement. It was automatic to step up. I really appreciated their dedication. I was definitely proud.

During the recovery experience at my sister's, I thought my days were over, but I was put back in the saddle. I was there at my older sister's home for two weeks, which was very helpful. I realized I had more work to do. The situation changed my life forever. After my wife's passing, I was in bad shape emotionally. I became a workaholic.

I realized that Hapkido class was more than just a business or a hobby. Spiritually, the sum total of these circumstances caused me to do a complete turnaround. It was also totally unexpected. I questioned myself: Should I have seen some signs? What could I have done better? Did I do something wrong? Did I not read the class properly? Hapkido is a life coach for some and a lifeline for others.

Hapkido is a protector for battered women. Hapkido is a family builder. I am forced to look at it in this manner after these tragic situations. I remembered the young man who had taken his life. He was a member of the class early in its development. The young man loved my class. He was there to say good-bye. A military investigator told me that, when someone makes up his or her mind like that, he or she is happy. He or she has made a decision.

I was so blown away by my experience. I went on a four-day retreat to Atlanta, where I heard some of the best gospel singers and preachers in the world. I had a worship experience! My divorce from Annie, her passing two years later, and this young man changed me for good.

I met a strong spiritual warrior on a trip with my church. Ever since then, my growth as a Christian has grown immeasurably. The scriptures took me to another level. I was ready! She was a minister. Boy, was she going to open my mind. She gave me some real medicine. This is a sample of what she gave me.

I was advised that this medicine must be taken with a cheerful heart. It must be taken at least three times a day. All instructions must be followed. The heart must be ministered to first. Next then, through faith, we will then travel along avenues where spirituality teaches, and I received them. Look closely. Everything happens for a reason.

P.S. This medicine must be taken internally. Put your seat belt on. Let's go to another level. We talked for one whole day at her place. She had given me a CD from a previous conference she'd had on healing. This is the prescription for healing on another level. This is what worked for me. I can't speak for everybody, but I can share my experiences with you. It's a testimony.

Yours may be different, but this is mine. We talked for hours. She gave me literature and a CD to listen too. I was so taken by it that I cried even now when I listen to the CD. Communications in many forms are valuable. It doesn't matter if it's word of mouth, CD, smartphone, or email. The Word is the Word.

During slavery it was unlawful to read. For those who learned to read, most often their first encounter with the written word might have been the Bible. However, it is possible through circumstance to know God. Everyone won't follow me here. It's all right.

Imagine if you learned one scripture verse. How and when would you use it? We bless our food by them. Sometimes we may give thanks by using them. We may use them as we say prayers at night. Would you sing your verse when you are happy? Oh, Lord, haven't we sung them? You would be surprised to find the number of gospel songs that originate from biblical verses. They are weapons or swords.

What about when you don't know what the future holds and are just happy for the moment? How do you express it? We have recited and used these verses in and out of church.

Here are a few. Make at least one yours, and let it minister to you and yours. There are many perversions in this life. How do we fight a spiritual battle? These verses will help in times of uncertainty.

- Psalms 27:1 (KJV): The lord is my light and my salvation; whom shall I fear? The Lord is the strength of my life: of whom shall I be afraid.
- Psalms 121:1 (KJV): Remember now thy Creator in the days of thy youth, while the evil days come not, nor the years draw nigh, when thou shalt say, I have no pleasure in them.
- Psalms 84:10 (KJV): For a day in thy courts is better than a thousand. I had rather be a doorkeeper in the house of my God, than to dwell in the tents of wickedness.

- Psalms 24:7 (KJV): Lift up your heads, O you gates; and be ye lift up, ye everlasting doors, and the King of glory shall come in.
- Psalms 27:14 (KJV): Wait on the Lord: be of good courage, and he will strengthen thine heart: wait, I say, on the Lord.
- Psalms 27:4 (KJV): One thing have I desired of the Lord, that will I seek after, that I may dwell in the house of the Lord all the days of my life, to behold the beauty of the Lord and to inquire in his temple.
- Psalms 30:5 (KJV): For his anger endured but a moment: In his favor is life: weeping may endure for a night, but joy comet in the morning.

It is important to realize that we do nothing by ourselves. I once looked at a wall of plaques, letters of appreciation, and medals and found that they meant absolutely nothing to anyone but me. What value did they have? I thought, *Should I throw them away? No. Should I keep them to remind me of who I was, am, or could be?* I was really a smaller I, and God was a big me. I sat looking at award after award. I had so many that I couldn't put them all on the wall.

I've learned that, at different points in life, we should leave markers. At certain points in life, we have turning points. At this point in my life, I experienced a turning point. I felt I must leave a marker. The physical warrior era had now passed.

I didn't need the gun anymore. I didn't have to prove anything to anybody. I had a track record. I could travel on my spirituality. I had graduated. The Word had become my bow and staff. The short stick was the biblical verses. Righteousness had become my rule and guide. Faith had become my shield. My feet were shod with peace. Now some of you should be feeling me.

Once a man or women learns about spiritually, he or she can learn to be triumphant in life and never lose a battle. Many may differ with what I just said, but this has been my experience. Spiritual warfare is on another level. Once you learn how to play and use the rules of the game, you will win every time you play.

When I learned that God was the larger and I was the smaller, I've been successful ever since I can remember. Is there a place in the martial arts for spirituality? I think there is if it is represented properly. In my opinion, everyone doesn't have to agree. We have free will. For me, spirituality is part of my very being.

I believe what a man soweth, so shall he reap. Can I teach you when you don't have confidence in me? If Muhammad Ali, one of the greatest athletes ever, can proclaim his faith, I can proclaim mine. Many people may disagree, but in my country, you have that right. The letters of appreciation are more valuable in many ways. The performances require levels of organization, correlation, and showmanship. They performed wonderfully.

I have worked with families and individuals trying to bring out the best in each person. Money is not a major player; nor it has ever been in my Hapkido program. It was always bigger than that. As time passed, the techniques I learned became as valuable as a family treasure, which was to be passed on to the next generation.

The older I get in life, the more I realize that certain things must be taught. For example, many American males are walking around, thinking they are men by birth. They don't realize, although they were born male, they have to be taught how to be a good one. They don't know how wrong they are. One must learn to follow rules in society so one can become a healthy citizen and a productive member.

Every game I ever played and every accomplishment I reached, I enjoyed every plaque, every medal, and every situation I was ever in. God was there. Without this knowledge, you can't run anything because you don't know the chain of command.

Every organization has a command structure, that is, the person who's in charge. Without this knowledge, how can you run a household? The things I have written above will seem odd and strange to some. For some, it will be musical.

If it is you, my family member, study it. I have learned that we must learn certain things on this journey. Some can take a lifetime to master. Everyone will not be ready to receive this at the time you read it. If God has blessed you and you understand as he has blessed me, hallelujah! If he hasn't got to you yet, ask. Blessings are for everyone.

The Ni Family (my adopted family)

What's happening? What is this all about? There are very few African American masters in Hapkido, to be frank. I don't know many. I met one on the West Coast once. I've heard of a few, but I don't know any.

This is something special I must recognize and be thankful for my experiences. By my marriage to a native South Korean, my instruction by the best in this field, and, for that matter, my being there, it is eye-opening.

The caliber of my instructors are in a foreign land. My military experiences and police experiences shaped my methodology. The levels I have achieved and the people I have helped and met is beyond my beliefs.

I never thought my hobby would end up being such a blessing. I started the class at this time over twenty years ago, and I'm having as much fun as ever. I was fortunate and blessed to learn overseas. I've never had an American instructor. They were all native South Koreans. The masters I met are legendary.

I learned in South Korea among the masters, which would later become my strongest trump card. I now realize that the South Korean culture and ethics have played a great part in my adult growth. My young adult life was shaped in South Korea. I had four tours there.

I also had the privilege of having the base commander at Kunsan AFB as a student in my martial arts class. He gathered the best Hapkidoist at that time in all of South Korea for truly authentic Hapkido demonstrations. This allowed us to experience the best of the best in the country.

This was another turning point in my growth as a martial artist. I saw the best in the country perform. That day I learned to be humble. I saw young masters at work on those demonstration teams.

Through time I've learned, the smaller I am, the larger I can become. There was a time when I thought I was a bigger and tougher than I was. Every accomplishment was a reason to take on a new challenge. What happens when you reach the top of the hill? Let's start again.

The church and Bible has always had a major influence on African American lives. The ministers were the most outspoken and respected members of our communities. Dr. Martin Luther King Jr. was a minister first. All that is not right can be corrected if we know who to ask. We as a people have come a long way. The church was the major vehicle.

I went to a funeral one time in which I saw a clear separation between the physical and the spiritual. Whatever was, it was no more. What was missing? It was evident the physical was present, but something was missing. It is important that every man, woman, and child attend at least one in life. Why? To see what I saw. That spiritual element of a person is absent. Every man, woman, and child is composed of the two elements: the spiritual and the physical. No matter what you believe, this is a cold fact.

To understand that we are made of the two is the first step toward knowing God. Without knowing God, a man cannot mature. How can he be the priest of his household without knowing there is someone greater than he is?

You are not a man. You can't run a household. You can't be a husband, wife, mother, or child until you get it right. You can't learn to love. You won't know what love is. It occurs in the heart before it becomes.

What is in a name? A name can be a badge of honor. It can be signs of a character that is possessed. It can be a hope of that which has yet to happen. Or it can be a promise to be fulfilled. It can be awarded for stupidity or bravery. It is what you are best known for.

The family name is one to be honored and respected. It's a place of dignity. Looking back on the many situations and issues that have shaped my life, I can cite many. Lundy is a good name. I've worked on it. (Smile.)

It has been said a man is known by his word. So when you said "My name is ...", that's a statement. There are thousands of people who have biblical names to remember the past struggles of mankind. What is your name? What does it say about you?

My students have called me Master Lundy. They mean Master Instructor Lundy. I realized to be promoted to master is not the same as your students recognizing you as a master instructor. You can't buy master. It's like the family name. A family name symbolizes a collective unity over time or generations. It's powerful!

It takes years of study, and it is a title earned and not to be taken lightly. I take this as a sign of respect. It has nothing to do with spiritually. These are my peers, and they have recognized me as a master of my craft. That means a lot!

I am just a man. They appreciate that I am one who has mastered his craft to a high degree. I am highly pleased that they call me a master of my craft, but let's not get it confused with Jesus Christ. I make it clear that my master is Jesus Christ and they can call me Mr. Lundy. The real master is Christ. I hope they see him in me.

If anybody asks you who I am, tell him or her that I'm a child of God. One Easter Sunday, I went to church, and this song was sung by a young woman no more than thirteen years of age. It struck me hard. I could not get it out of my mind. A couple weeks passed, and one of my daughters asked me the question, "What is our real name?"

Then I thought, if anybody asks me who I am, I'm telling him or her that I'm a child of God. All of the other things I had no control over doesn't matter. Please pass this message on. This is another attempt. I'm trying to explain what happened.

One time a family support group on base asked me to put on a demonstration for about sixty family members. I don't charge for these types of outings. I just ask that my students and I receive letters of appreciation. This group of family members was losing their dad for a few months and needed something for the family to do collectively. It was less of a burden on one parent.

While their husbands were deployed to overseas locations, they kept busy. They were all military members. They had younger members. The ages varied. I was determined to keep them together. What a challenge. I, as they, was extremely happy. We enjoyed working together.

One day, they, in return, put on a demonstration for another group. I had arranged for them to receive certificates of appreciation for their support. I never ask for money during demonstrations.

Sometimes families don't complete the course. For a time, Dad or Mom are joined together for a while as a family. I create with the combative art form, but the love and the camaraderie we experience can be a healer. Love it.

The police academy was a special time. I met some good people. I found it was a very political position. It was very competitive and restrictive. Promotion was very hard to obtain. This is especially true if you are with a small department.

At the same time, I had a business with Langley AFB as a civilian contractor. I was a martial arts instructor. I had been scheduled to attend the academy for a self-defense instructor. For some reason, it was canceled four times. Well, it was not to be. I continue to teach outside the workplace at Langley. Many appreciated me.

At one time, my class was attracting mothers and sons, and then there were fathers and sons. There were fathers who wanted something they could do with their sons. There were a couple moms who brought their sons there but didn't participate in the class, but they liked the idea of their sons participating in the class.

I remember one situation very well. A father and son started together, and the son later ended up getting married to one of the female members. Dad did not finish the course, but Junior found someone he liked better than hanging out with Dad. The couple finished the course and are now park rangers in Hampton.

There was a time in my life where, as a Hapkidoist, I made a complete spiritual turn. In the late 1980s, while serving at Langley AFB, one of my students, a fifteen-year-old member, committed suicide. The situation changed my life forever and sent me to another level in life spiritually.

I had a good-sized class of teenage youth, young sailors, and airmen. Two were females. One was a military dependent youth in her teens. The other was from the Netherlands, a dependent wife who spoke five languages, which I thought was interesting. This class had the greatest impact on me.

I didn't miss class often. I found my students valued them greatly. Sometimes until this day, we hold classes on Christmas Eve. We exchange gifts among each other through a drawing. I'm headed for uncharted ground. I remembered my time at Minot my last time.

Minot! It was a twenty-year journey and back to my first assignment in the air force. I spent thirty days home and then went off to Minot by myself with no family. This was the last tour in uniform. As I stood in the commander's office at Minot, he informed me that I had been handpicked for this assignment. Really!

I was to be one of the flight chief of an intercontinental missile security flight. There were two of us. Our job was special as a tactical response team for the security of a number of nuclear missile sites and their alarm systems. My job was to maintain security and perform recovery operations. That means I was expendable. I was a master sergeant now.

Another promotion had made master sergeant. That was my sixth stripe en route to Minot. The commander told me that they needed me. The unit had two suicides among the troops in the past two months. They needed a man like me to work in the field. It was flattering, but I had issues too. I had been away from home for the second year in a row. Thank God he strengthened me. Would I have a marriage when I got back?

I endured some very lonely and painful nights at Minot for the second time. I had to keep occupied. I sang in the church choir. I just showed up one Monday and started singing. I knew I needed the support of a church family. They took me, and I have been singing until today.

I enjoyed singing and preparing to sing the songs. I met some people whom I will never forget. I met some old friends who enforced my faith. A couple from the Philippines was a family away from home. They had known Annie and me in the Philippines. They now had a family of five.

Circumstances had taken a toll on my marriage. I had to support two households. I called home weekly. I tried to keep up with the children's grades. My heart ached.

Hapkido has become now a vehicle for social chance. About-face! Learning to be an honorable man is one of these tasks. It is possible for a man to become a spiritual warrior before he experiences the physical act.

Learning to be a man involves how to treat the opposite sex. This is an area that must be learned, preferably at home. Some of the lifelong lessons is learning to treat a woman with respect even when you disagree. Go to the prom! Why?

I didn't go to my prom growing up. I thought I was too cool to go to the school prom. Growing up in a metropolitan might have made a big difference. In New York City, two or three hundred seniors can easily be the class. In a rural community, this may not be an issue. Then think if all your dates are your relatives.

I have learned to regret that I didn't go. That prom had some valuable lessons. Take someone of the opposite sex. Take your mom or dad, but not both if you have to. It could take a lifetime to repeat these experiences. Experience is the best teachers.

This is your first time at a young age where you take a member of the opposite sex out socially, that is, if you have earned the privilege, being responsible enough to reach an educational level in school where everyone is proud of you. It's your training ground.

Treat her like a lady. For a young man or woman, this might be the first social outing he or she shares with the opposite sex formally. I realize a lot of life's lessons can be learned this night.

Learn to tie a tie. Always wear clean drawers or underwear when you can, especially when you are traveling. This was a big joke in my house when Mom talked about medical assistance and the doctor. Learn to dress like you are going for an interview.

The prom is a good place to work out most of these activities. One of my students bought the first suit of his young life for this purpose. I wonder how long it would have taken if he didn't go to that prom. He was fourteen. Have you went, and are you going?

Learning to dress for the prom can be a valuable experience. Think about it. When I finished, the military part of our debriefing was knowing how to dress for an interview when looking for a job, for example, when to get a black or dark blue suit for special and formal occasions.

Wear at least one pair of lace-up shoes, black or brown. Ladies, it's the same. Don't wear skirts above the knee or low-cut blouses. Dress conservatively or appropriately to the position you are attempting to get. It took me twenty-plus years to learn this one. It was at my retirement outbriefing from the military.

Learn to treat the host, hostess, waiter, or waitress with respect. You don't own him or her. Most people forget they bring your food. I had to learn this the hard way. Thank God I'm still alive.

Having been a police officer at certain restaurants, you could receive meals for free. Sometimes some of the people you've locked up or their relatives are serving or preparing the food. Be careful where you eat. Always know who is feeding you.

111

As a member of the martial arts community, I believe that my students are a part of one big family. My attitude as an instructor can influence people for a lifetime. I value being a role model and mentor to my students, and I take it very seriously. I would like my family to be physically fit, mentally strong, and morally grounded.

I have one large Hapkido family, my class at Kunsan AFB, and the South Korean members of some local schools. Learning to have a genuine love of others is a tall order, but in my opinion, it's an honorable one. This goal may not be accomplished in all areas, but a good try is always better than doing nothing.

The smiles of approval are fascinating, and the confidence they exude, you can see it smoking out of their heads. I've truly become a martial artist. I can teach a six-year-old and a sixty-year-old person at the same time and wrap the art around them like a suit of well-fit clothes, like an artist creates on canvas.

What was the problem? The male ego would not allow most men to accept that women can handle them easily. In some cases, it is against cultural etiquette. How much should the women know? How must defense is she allowed to know? Is the male ego equipped to accept the fact that he doesn't need to protect her physically?

I was once told, because my daughters were so beautiful, I should not mess them up by teaching them to handle themselves. They took their looks from their mother. They got personality from me, I think. It was said they may never get a boyfriend if I continued to teach them this most effective skill. I must say, in some cases, this might be true. It made sense. I didn't push them.

I took it to heart. I will only teach them if they desired. I know one thing. Whenever I had females in the class, the class doubled in size. The females make better martial artists than the guys do. The females rely on technique and not strength. It takes about six months to teach the guys that it's technique and not strength that is most effective.

I pray they will see me and like me as a person. I would like my students to realize that I'm a Christian first and that God is the wind beneath my sail. When we are Christians, there is always hope. That is my message. Hapkido can be an instrument, but God is the main source. I hope they can see him in me. Hapkido has been my platform all these years.

The hip throw, technique number eight, is where, as you fall forward, you will land right in front. A trained practitioner can survive a fall or throw like this without injury.

Chapter eight was full of situations that were surprising to me. It was called the hip throw. You know where you are falling. The family I mentioned, the ones I gave the hundred dollars to, contacted me years later. I was surprised when they sent me a picture of their firstborn. I can see him in the future in a little Hapkido uniform. We never know where we might land. God bless the three of you guys, wherever you are.

Chapter 9 is the neck breaker.

THE NECK BREAKER

Technique #9

The Journey

Mr. Myung and me first meeting at Langley AFB

There was a time when I thought I was running things. I often thought my destiny was of my making, but several incidents made me realize that was not so. There were too many coincidences. This is spiritually, whether others believe it or not.

The South Korean masters I'd studied under the many trips to South Korea was not an accident. I never had an American instructor. I learned from men who had spent their entire lives studying Hapkido.

With my marriage to a South Korean spouse, I think it helped me to be accepted culturally. My being able to teach at the base in South Korea as the head student on many occasions added to my confidence. My understanding of the Korean language, my marriage, and my position was all God's doing. He had raised me to a very high ranking among Hapkidoists. In South Korea and the United States, I had good credentials. I was placed in a position to serve others.

Later I always looked for teachable moments to make leaders out of my students. I applaud Masters Pak and Kim in South Korea and Grandmasters Jae and Myung Kwang Sik in America. All of these guys were native South Koreans.

In now over twenty years, I have not seen another African American who has been promoted to the level I have been accredited with. How did this happen? I'm blessed. Although there may be some, I have not heard or seen them in over twenty years. Hapkido has become more than a physical combative art form for me.

In my later years, certifications and paper trails have become very important. Many people can produce first-degree paperwork, but who has promoted you to the upper levels besides yourself?

We are not in South Korea with governmental martial arts programs. We must look for certified people to award certifications to good practitioners. If not, we can easily wind up with Kool-Aid instead of good technique.

Grandmaster Kwang Sik Myung was a student of the legendary grandmaster, Ji Han Jae. Grandmaster Jae was once the head of the Korea Hapkido Association. The most famous of all the modern-day Hapkioist, Grandmaster Jae was once a presidential bodyguard for the president of South Korea. In South Korea, a grandmaster is licensed by the government and labeled the best in the country. Grandmaster Jae held that position.

Mr. Pak and Grandmaster Myung were all presidents of the Korean Hapkido Association, a high honor. He was influenced by perhaps the father of Hapkido, who many say was influenced by a Japanese Aikido master. Hapkido is rooted in the grappling styles and has evolved over a period of time. I can't speak for what I didn't see, but in my lifetime, this is what I have learned about its history.

On my first-degree paperwork, it was signed by Mr. Jae as the president of the Korean Hapkido Association. Mr. Pak was my master instructor there, but he endorsed it. Mr. Pak later became president of the Korean Hapkido Association, definitely a high point in his life. These titles meant a lot to these men because they were licensed by the government of South Korea.

A track record has been established between the students and the teachers. This is important when you are in highly competitive situations. In the Orient, martial arts can be big business as well as a symbol of cultural pride.

I lost track with Mr. Pak when he moved to Seoul on my third trip. The last time I saw him was in Osan. I respect him and am thankful for him sharing his love of this art form with me.

My mentor Mr. Pak used to say one time, "Finishee." He meant to execute with tenacity or "Ki" with every technique. The combination of using the Ki technique in Hapkido is a powerful one. Faith is also an element that can trump both.

I have found many similarities with the Japanese Aikido system. However, the kicking system is totally and without a doubt South Korean. South Koreans are famous for their kicking ability. The elements of pressure points and the concept of concentrated power has evolved into modern-day Hapkido.

Traditional South Korean martial arts has had an influence with the weapons application of the techniques. My experience was the "O brothers" in Kunsan. They were famous for their use of the wooden staff, swords, canes, and short sticks along with ropes. On the higher levels, the weapons become extensions of your hands. Culturally they definitely had significance. Hapkido is sometimes called the royal court martial art. This is because of the advanced techniques taught.

In times past, these techniques were only taught to nobility. Imagine an army put in the field with these types of combative skills. Imagine their combative skills with weapons. It makes you proud of your cultural heritage.

I also was influenced by Master Kim in Daegu, South Korea. This was a traditional and softer version of the grappling styles. It was called KuK Sool Won then. Today at Kunsan, it's called KuK Sool Hapkido.

We must remember these instructors are all South Korean. They will choose the most effective techniques in a style. I understand that only the best techniques will survive. South Korea has over a three thousand-year history.

Any of us will agree that Hapkido has evolved over the years. Grandmaster Myung has documented these techniques on videos and books. (See selective readings or viewing in this case.) However, there is no substitute for an experienced instructor.

See his series under the World Hapkido Federation series of tapes on Hapkido. Look under my selective viewing section. They can be used to guide an individual, but there is no substitute for the watchful eye of a trained instructor.

Most people will view the tapes and falsely think they know the techniques. They may be wrong. Also there is a reasonable sequence in learning the techniques. Next a highly trained instructor can advise on safety. Hapkido is hard to teach if you don't know the basics.

One other reason to search for capable instruction is to keep the integrity of the style. Another reason is how a good instructor can save valuable instruction time. Often a good instructor can see the connections between traditional and contemporary technique.

It should not take a master years to instruct potential beginning students to make first-degree black belt. Don't get me wrong. Hapkido can be a lifetime's work. This might be a warning sign when choosing a suitable instructor.

Grandmaster Myung has done more to document the structure according to his teachings than anyone I know. Grandmaster Myung promoted me to third-, fourth-, and fifth-degree black belt holder. He has over two hundred schools under his federation and was located in thirty foreign countries at one time. Grandmaster Myung has been my mentor for more than twenty years. I attended seminars in Los Angles. Mr. Myung visited my class a couple times over the years at Langley.

I progressed through his leadership and watch. He endorsed my paperwork proudly. I have found him to be truly an honorable man. I visited him a couple times. The last time was in 1999. I received my fifth degree from him.

Mr. Myung endorsed my third, fourth, and fifth degree. Even today I'm happy to have encountered such a talent. I must truly say I have been blessed.

Technique number nine is titled the "neck breaker." Mr. Pak used to say, "One time Fineeeeee." This meant one effort. "Hap" means "to coordinate." "Ki" means "the power of." And "Do" means "the art of." Hapkido is the art of coordinated power. This is what he meant. Every technique was to be performed using this concept, with intensity, as I understood it.

Circular motion, the water principle, and nonresistance are the other elements of the Hapkido philosophy. My students will remember this technique as being the ninth technique in our system.

The Hapkido system has thousands of variables. A South Korean Hapkido master, a family friend's father, once told me that you are a master when you recognize there is only ten. I was instructing his son. I was a second degree then.

I learned that these ten techniques, as once described to me, made me a master instructor over the years. I found the hundreds of techniques. I had learned there was only ten. These first ten in my case had brought the student back time and time again. They were so impressive.

Years have passed. I've had students coming to be to be taught for over thirty years. There came a point where people were just showing up for study. I found the best advertisement was word of mouth.

I realize that, according to Mr. Myung, the Hapkido structure had 270 major techniques with the possibility of over ten thousand variables. This structure makes for a very rich and strong structure. With this blueprint, you can study for years.

Hapkido builds on these structures. Therefore, it is very important that the practitioner developed a good background. The structure has a progression that includes empty hand techniques against empty hand.

The next platform is empty hand against weapons. At its apex, weapon against weapon using the learned techniques are all inclusive. The system builds on itself.

The final lesson I have learned from the South Koreans required that you have an attitude of optimism. The Japanese and Koreans call it "Ki." The Chinese call it "Chi." This concept of succeeding at all cost would be in my blood. One time Finishee!

Treat every opportunity like it is your last. What I remember most from this group of professionals was that one of my students was a surgeon. He confirmed all of my beliefs I had learned from the masters. He confirmed that these techniques would cause the damage I had been trained to inflict. He had been professionally trained.

Be the best you can be in life. To Doc, Curtis, Steve, the Taylors, and the Osbornes, I hope you guys are teaching. This is the spirit of Hapkido.

The final technique is what we call the reverse hip throw. This concludes the ten chapters in *Master Lundy's Hapkido*. This is my view as a master instructor.

I realize that Asian culture shaped my young adult life, my prime. These people shaped my late teens through manhood. I thank them for taking good care and teaching me lessons I could treasure for life. Read on!

CHAPTER 10

THE REVERSE HIP THROW

Technique #10

The Master's Touch
Where Will I Land?

My service picture (Service)

The reverse hip throw was a technique where you used your hip to throw your opponent backward. By landing backward, you can do two things: brace yourself for the fall or hold on. I have an interesting story in closing that I would like to share with you. It started while I was writing this book. 9/11 was a difficult time for us as Americans.

As a career serviceman, I wondered what if I were in Iraq, serving for Iraqi freedom. When I returned home, I found family and relatives asking if I were from Louisiana, missing with no records of the family. Wow!

This was the beginning of my literary career. The Bible taught me how to know and speak to God. I learned about the many pieces of fabric that are in our society. Hapkido has shown me how to master some physical challenges in society. However, it was the forerunner to a study of spiritual warfare that I have encountered in my later years as a senior citizen.

We tend to ask what life is all about. Most times when you are over fifty years of age, you realize you might have more years behind you than in front of you. If you have problems with the math, just double your present age.

I, now as an adult and parent, realize that all of that was necessary to make me who and whatever I am today. You see, for good or bad, you will become the sum total of your life experiences. It is important for you to learn to honor your parents and realize why you do or don't need them. Sometimes things don't work out like we would expect, but always be aware that things happen for a reason.

Everyone has different feelings and emotions. This is what makes a good flower garden. One thing for sure is that a seed is a seed. You may be more like your parents than you think.

The whole family was able to fit under one tent hapkido. For the family on Langley where the father was deployed overseas, we used hapkido as a unifier. Thank you, guys. I will never forget you. Michael, I hope you are still kicking strong.

I now realize that my children were a gift that I was to take care of for a while until they were strong enough to handle life's ups and downs. I realize they were mine for a while, but they belonged to God. And when they found that out, they could handle things on their own.

Who can take care of them better than me, God? Generation X is your responsibility. The millenials, as the youth of today are called, are community property. It's the whole country's responsibility to ensure they are nurtured properly.

Maybe children were born to teach adults how to love. No matter what you do, parents will always love you, no matter what the circumstances. A seed is a seed. Jealousy, envy, hurt, and anger are teaching tools. They are like fire. If you hold on, they will burn you. We should always treasure and love the youth of society. Sometimes tough love is needed. Just remember sometimes adults are still growing too.

We are not the same from season to season. Just remember. From time to time, when things gets rough, remind us that you love us and we love you … signed the grown-ups. Over the years I've learned to teach students from six years old to sixty. Some of us, including me, are forever children at heart.

Hapkido has become my platform, my grandstand in life. Everyone has his or her unique parts of his or her character, of which God uses to glorify and edify. Hapkido was my root that God used to feed me.

Hapkido was and is my platform. This has made me a better father. I hope my two lovely daughters, Angie and Freda, both government workers, learn to serve their fellow man, as I have and be something special to someone else. I see it in them already. Thank you, Jesus. I'm thankful for such bright and ambitious young women. Your mom did a good job. Also may she rest in peace.

I'm proud to say that they are my children. They don't know how much they have meant to be. I had to do what was morally acceptable because my future grandchildren would suffer. I'm looking for some grandkids under the right conditions. (Smile.) Thanks to their mother whom I loved dearly and her people who played such a pivotal role in my life. Thank God for protecting and giving me the wisdom to be a good father and parent.

The Majors are a family of Hapkidoist and good ones! Kyra won't forget.

My students respected me as an instructor and mentor. They were destined to find that I was a Christian. That was one of my strongest qualities.

This was my Hapkido with a master's touch, the hand of God. The transformation occurred slowly but masterfully. Over the years, training as a martial arts instructor has prepared me for physical warfare.

God prepared me for spiritual warfare. Over the years, I became a spiritual warrior. My accomplishments as a martial artist are nothing in relationship to the thousands of lessons God has taught me. Hapkido was my instrument. God was my pilot. I cherish every class that he has provided me with. I thank him for the great instructors he led me to. Thanks for the saints he placed in my life to guide me. It was a setup.

It was God, I believe, who turned me from a physical warrior to a spiritual one. The question was, "Master Lundy, how do you fight a spiritual battle?" I realize this was a different type of battle and required different tools and weapons. Ephesians 6 (KJV) will support this thought. My spiritual growth was done so cleverly and with such grace that it had a master's touch.

It's my hope that *Master Lundy's Hapkido* becomes your Hapkido. This is not the end of the story, but for now, I think I have said enough. Hapkido is not my God, but my God used it as an instrument in my opinion.

Thank God! To God is the glory. I am forever grateful.

KEYWORD LIST

black belt
blog
book
certification
Christian
first degree
Gi Han Jae
Hapkido blog
Hapkido master
Hapkido structure
Kuk Sul Won
Kunsan, South Korea
Langley Hapkido Club
Lundy
Master Lundy's website
Myung Kwang Sik
Pak Son Han
promotion
rank
Sin Moo Hapkido
soldier's story
South Korea
Traditional Hapkido
website

SELECTIVE READING

Jakes, T. D. *Instinct*. T. D. Jakes Enterprises, LLP: 2014.

Life Application Bible. Tyndale House Publications: 1988, 1989, 1990.

Myung Kwang Sik. *Korean Hapkido*. Seoul: 1967, 1986.

———. *Special Self-Protection Techniques*. South Korea: Seolim Publishing Company, 1993.

———. *The Cane Technique*, vol. 1. San Mun Printing Company: 1988.

———. *The Knife Technique*, vol. 11. 1988.

———. *Hyung Sae Techniques*, vol. 111. 1988.

Sharpton, Rev. Al. *The Rejected Stone*. 2013.

Tedeschi, Marc. *Hapkido Traditions*: Philosophy, Technique. Weather Hill, Inc.: 2000.

WORD LIST

African American Hapkido master
books
Carlton Lundy
certification
endorsement fifth degree
first degree
Founder, Langley Hapkido
Kunsan, South Korea
master
Master Carlton Lundy
Military/Hapkido US Air Force Hapkido
promotion
security specialist
traditional Hapkido
US Air Force
Website, Traditional Hapkido
World Hapkido Federation

IMAGES

Banana tree in the front yard Philippines,
Clark airbase one morning

Master Pak and members of International
Hapkido Team, Kunsan

I and new hires to Hampton Police in Virginia

Membership in the WHF

Minot class, North Dakota AFB

My first degree black belt endorsed by
Grandmaster Jae in South Korea

My first assignment, Minot AFB, ND B-52s

Commonwealth of Virginia

Department of Criminal Justice Services

This will acknowledge that

Carlton Lundy

has met the minimum employment and training requirements
as established within the Commonwealth of Virginia for

Law Enforcement Officer Certification

in accordance with Section 15.1-131.8:1 of the Code of Virginia

August 30, 1996

ISSUE DATE

NT OF CRIMINAL
E SERVICES

My law enforcement certification

Myself and Grandmaster Myung, Tustin, California
(founder of World Hapkido Federation)

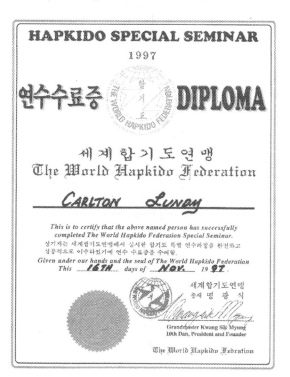

WHF seminar diploma

My last assignment at Kunsan AFB

Main Gate Kunsan AFB South Korea

Last enlistment in the United States Air Force

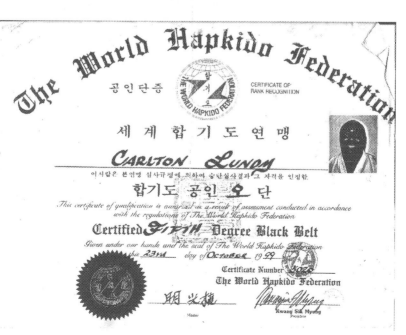

5th degree, promoted by Grand Master
Myung (Head of WHF) 1999

Rice fields in South Korea

Winter time at Minot AFB

ABOUT THE AUTHOR

I have personally trained and promoted over forty black belt holders. I'm the founder of the first traditional Hapkido Club at Langley Air Force Base (AFB) in Virginia. I'm one of the few African American Hapkido masters in the United States. The founder of the World Hapkido Federation, Myung Kwang Sik, promoted me to fifth degree in 1999.

Printed in the United States
By Bookmasters